God's House, Our Home

JOHN D. KENNINGTON

Essence
PUBLISHING

Belleville, Ontario, Canada

GOD'S HOUSE, OUR HOME

Copyright © 2002, John D. Kennington

Scriptures quotations, unless otherwise marked, are taken from *The Holy Bible, New International Version* ®. Copyright © 1973, 1978, 1984 by International Bible Society. Used by permission of Zondervan Publishing House. All rights reserved

All Scripture quotations marked KJV are from *The Holy Bible, King James Version.* Copyright © 1977, 1984, Thomas Nelson Inc., Publishers.

Notes in brackets within the Bible text are the author's emphasis, comments and clarifications.

ISBN: 1-55306-372-4

Essence Publishing is a Christian Book Publisher dedicated to further-ing the work of Christ through the written word. For more information, contact: 44 Moira Street West, Belleville, Ontario, Canada K8P 1S3.
Phone: 1-800-238-6376. Fax: (613) 962-3055.
E-mail: info@essencegroup.com
Internet: www.essencegroup.com

Printed in Canada
by

Essence
PUBLISHING

TABLE OF CONTENTS

PREFACE

*Approximately one third of the people in the
United States are unchurched.... Ten million
of these say they are born again.*[1]

These shocking statistics show that many Christians
have little biblical understanding of churches and of
the role God has assigned them. These unchurched people
are the spiritually homeless, and they are similar to the
physically homeless who prefer to live outside of what they
perceive as the establishment. Most of us are acquainted
with some "homeless Christians" who have no support
group, whose families to a great extent are not under the
influence of Christ, and who are not functioning as a part
of the "team."

This needy group is one of the reasons I feel compelled
to write. It is my purpose, by a simple straightforward
approach, to take this subject off the top shelf of theological
thinking and put it within the reach of ordinary readers, the
people who need it most and for whom it can make the
biggest difference. I am not writing for the scholar, partly
because I am only a student and not a scholar myself. I have,

however, read the scholars, as the reader will see from the many quotes herein. I am writing for the student who is interested enough to read and think for himself.

Many are more capable than I to write on this subject, and I hope that this book will stir those more capable to devote their scholarship to this theme which can have a transforming effect on ministers and laymen alike. I only wish that, as a young pastor, I could have had this material available to me as I ventured forth on my pastoral journey.

Our journey is through familiar territory and its purpose is to focus on things which the reader may have overlooked. The United States Lines, a cruise-ship line promoting a Hawaiian cruise, said in a recent ad, "Never seen Hawaii? Don't worry. Neither have most of the folks who've been there." The same is true of the multitudes who have been in church most of their lives. They still haven't had the help of a guide to point out many glorious and wonderful views of the Church as seen in Scripture.

The maze of religious organizations claiming to be the correct one so bewilder many, they don't bother to devote much time to investigate the form and function of the New Testament Church. Some say, "Leave it to the scholars," but this removes the Bible from the hands of ordinary Christians and puts us under a kind of intellectual priestcraft. Meanwhile, others opt for submitting to what appears to have the most historical validity. Many would rather just forget it and busy themselves for Christ wherever they are. But, most regrettably, large numbers just withdraw and don't seriously participate in any church life. Some even suggest that the Bible really has no clear teaching on this subject, and that we are simply left to do what seems best in any particular situation.

Elizabeth Elliott quotes her to-be-martyred husband, Jim, about this "anything will do" attitude. He said,

> The pivot point hangs on whether or not God has revealed a universal pattern for the church in the New Testament. If He has not, then anything will do so long as it works. But I am convinced that nothing so dear to the heart of Christ as his Bride should be left without explicit instructions as to her corporate conduct. I am further convinced that the twentieth century has in no way simulated this pattern in its method of "churching" a community…. Further, it matters not at all to me what men have done with the Church over there or in America; it is incumbent upon me, if God has a pattern for the Church, to find and establish that pattern at all costs.[2]

Do divisions within Christendom bother you? Many are conscience stricken over the divisions amongst Christians. Some would solve this by returning to the "mother church," meaning Rome, or would seek verification of their validity in the pages of history. Others have taken the ecumenical route, and to do so, have opted for the lowest common denominator, thus reducing much of the Bible to a point of irrelevance. Yet a simple return to the pattern of the autonomy of the local church opens the way for a recognition of, and a cooperation with, the rest of our fellow Christians. There is a simple way out of competitive Christianity. We need not be involved with the control, coercion, and politics that blight Christendom today.

A scriptural approach can assure you and your church of an authentic identity and provide the kind of environment that results in spiritual growth. This keeps us from being a part of the spiritual nomads who drift from church to church, never maturing enough to accept the responsibility that is consistent with being a Christian.

Probably the most significant thing of all is that the churches, by returning to the simplicity and pattern of the early Church, can recover their apostolic mission of working together to fulfill the Great Commission without all the duplication of efforts and organization. There is nothing so efficient as when all the local churches become missionary outposts.

I want to thank all who assisted in the preparation of this manuscript, particularly Pat Johnson, who worked tirelessly, using both her computer and editorial skills. Also, Erik Persson, who did some of the initial editing, and Beth Nance, who contributed much to the chapter on the "Mission of the Local Church" as well as providing guidance throughout the book. Also, I am deeply indebted to over 200 pastors who critiqued these pages and contributed valuable input.

～ NOTES

[1] The Barna Research Group. *Our Church*. April/June 2000.
[2] Elliott. *Shadow of the Almighty*. 139.

INTRODUCTION

Which church did Jesus found? Which one is right? How important is it anyway? The answers to these and many more questions are dependent on the source to whom you are listening.

Divisions amongst the people of God cannot be ignored. What people have done to one another or said of each other while contending for the title of the "true" church is a dreadful stain on Church history. Some have gone so far as to claim there is no salvation outside their organization, and others, while not saying as much, have behaved as though they had exclusive distribution rights to the gospel. Many have built high fences around their particular organization to keep their sheep "in the fold." Many ministers are compelled to sign statements of faith annually to show they haven't deviated from their religious party line.

Claims to being the authentic church have been based on historical continuity, certain sacraments, or on a particular interpretation of the Scripture. Some seem to have even made an exclusive claim on the name of Jesus. Many others have just opted for a pragmatic approach and, in doing so, say that our Lord has left it up to us to find the best way to function within diverse cultures. Often churches simply mirror their society, modeling their structure after the business world.

Once, when traveling on a train, I encountered a clergy-man from a certain organization that claimed one had to a part of his denomination to be saved. When I asked him where I fit in since I had simply responded to the gospel as found in the Gospel of John, committed my life to Christ, and, as a result, experienced a new life in Christ. I questioned, "Whom shall I believe, Jesus or your denomination?"

He replied, "Both, for we recognize you as a Christian; you must belong to the 'soul' of our denomination even though you are not a part of its body."

How do you resolve such differences? Consider this contrast: In ancient times there was one king who had a beautiful man-made lake in front of his palace. It reflected the image of his palace. I believe this is an apt illustration of how Jesus wants his Church to reflect Christ's throne and not the society around it.

Do you believe the Lord was simply trying to confuse us about such an important issue? Is there a simplicity in the pattern given to us by our Lord that is lost while we orga-nize structure? Is it possible we have complicated the sub-ject by imposing our own preconceptions on his churches? Have our sinful tendencies contaminated the simplicity and purity of his plan?

DEFINITION OF A LOCAL CHURCH

What did our Lord mean by a "church"? What was its form to be? Here is an interesting extract from what is called "The Scot's Confession":

The notes of the true Kirk [church], we believe, con-fess, and avowe to be: first the true preaching of the

Word of God, in which God has revealed himself to us, as the writings of the prophets and apostles declare; secondly the right administration of the sacraments of Christ Jesus… and lastly, ecclesiastical discipline uprightly ministered….

This is not unlike the conclusion to which I have come, which is this: A church is a body of people called together by his gospel, gathered in the presence of the Lord, committed to him as their Lord and to the company called and gathered unto him. This body of people has a three-fold purpose: 1) to glorify the Lord; 2) to encourage and edify each other; and 3) to fulfill the Great Commission.

In principle this harmonizes with a voice of the past when Ignatius wrote, in the second century A.D., "Where Christ is, there is the Church," and, "Ever since the Council of Constantinople in A.D. 381 Christians have confessed that the true church is one, holy, catholic and apostolic."[1]

How do I interpret terms like "holy," "catholic," and "apostolic"? "Holy" means a people set apart for God; "catholic" means that each church is one with all true churches and inclusive of all races and classes of people; and "apostolic" means both a commitment to the teachings of the apostles and an involvement in the apostolic mission of fulfilling Christ's commission to disciple all nations.

Consider the following:

1. *Our Lord is the architect of the Church and the churches he is building;*

2. *as architects often do, our Architect has given us some pictures of the building he is erecting;*

3. *he has given us some clear guiding principles that have proven workable throughout Church history;*

4. *he has made some very strong statements about our relationships to one another which must not be violated;*

5. *when Jesus chartered the first local church, his words clearly implied many of the essential elements of a church.*

JESUS WALKS IN THE MIDST OF LOCAL CHURCHES

"I walk today where Jesus walks, not where Jesus walked yesterday," said Pastor E.C. Erickson to a younger pastor, telling of his planned visit to Israel. Pastor Erickson based his comment on the eloquent picture painted in Jesus' revelation to the angel of the church in Ephesus: *"These are the words of him who holds the seven stars in his right hand and walks among the seven golden lampstands"* (Rev. 2:1).[2] Let's consider the churches depicted by these lampstands.

This visualization of local churches as "golden lampstands" graphically portrays the importance of these churches as lights in their given areas and their relationship to their risen Lord and to one another. This, in my opinion, implies a form of church government as well as how these churches are to relate to each other. Surely this "picture" is worth the proverbial thousand words as it portrays the significance of each local church and how they are to relate to Christ and to each other.

The following exhortation, *"He who has an ear, let him hear what the Spirit says to the churches"* (Rev. 2:29), helps us see the pattern of corporate Christianity and beyond the individualism plaguing Christianity today. Each one of us needs an authentic experience of corporate Christian life for our normal development.

We encounter this same high view of the churches depicted in Revelation in the apostle Paul's exhortation to the elders in the church at Ephesus:

> *Keep watch over yourselves and all the flock of which the Holy Spirit has made you overseers* [bishops]. *Be shepherds* [pastors] *of the church of God, which he bought with his own blood"* (Acts 20:28) [emphasis mine].

The "church" bought by God's blood to which Paul referred was the local church at Ephesus, for these elders weren't overseeing any universal Church. What is said about the universal Church applies to a local church. Christ loved the Church; he loves the Church. He loves *your* church.

> *...Christ loved the church and gave himself up for her to make her holy, cleansing her by the washing with water through the word* (Eph. 5:25).

The Church that Jesus loves is not a perfect Church. *"...God demonstrates his own love for us in this: While we were yet sinners, Christ died for us"* (Rom. 5:8). So his love is not based on perfection. Sometimes we excuse ourselves for not loving the Church because of all the imperfections we see in it. Then we are out of step with the Lord Jesus, who loves the Church unconditionally. To truly love the Lord is to truly love the Church which Jesus loves. He loves your church and calls you to love it, too.

Everyone whom the Lord saves, he adds to the Church. *"...And the Lord added to their number daily those who were being saved"* (Acts 2:47). They weren't saved by being added to the Church; but rather, all being saved were added. Everyone needs to participate in a church to continue the ongoing process of salvation after having experienced Christ's saving grace. The Church is for our good and not merely for the good of the leaders or the organization. It is a place where we are to be equipped for service.

When Billy Graham had an outstanding crusade in Los Angeles, California, he was criticized for saying that "he had set Christian work back by a hundred years or more." Graham answered, "I had hoped to set it back about two thousand years." In fact, he had hoped to recapture the dynamics of the early Church.

This helps us to see the significance of the early Church. Such a "setback" requires a return to the significance of the local churches and to their apostolic mission. It is my belief that the dynamics of the early Church cannot be realized without breaking out of the structures of traditional organizations found in many denominations.

My purpose in writing this book is to help move today's church life more toward the simplicity of the early Church. By this, I mean both to the form and function of autonomous churches. I will seek to show that such local churches are biblical, universal (catholic), historical, and viable. Such churches can be inclusive, fulfilling, and effective missionary organizations.

Over fifty years of experience in the pastorate has given me an ever-increasing burden for the local church and involved me with extensive reading in this field. In the process, many passages of Scripture have come into focus. Much has been learned as I have faced my own mistakes and sought answers from Scripture.

I would like to ignite your heart with a fire like that

which burns in mine, a fire fueled by the spiritual facts that local churches are "the holy ground" of his presence, the end of a pilgrimage, for he is there. May each of us end up saying, like Jacob of old:

> *Surely the Lord is in this place…. How awesome is this place! This is none other than the house of God; this is the gate of heaven* (Gen. 28:16,17).

This may have been the apostle Paul's inspiration when he said the local church is *"God's household, which is the church of the living God, the pillar and foundation of the truth"* (1 Tim. 3:15). These words free us from defining a church by size or magnificent architecture. They are temples made of living stones (1 Pet. 2:5), God's very habitation. This lifts us beyond programs and personalities to a preoccupation with our blessed Lord so that we may go in and sit before the Lord, as David did (2 Sam. 7:18).

METHODOLOGY

Since I believe in the sufficiency of the Scripture, my methodology is intended to do the following:

1. *state the clear implications of Jesus' words when he first mentioned the local church in Matthew 18;*
2. *set out the examples of what constituted a church;*
3. *show how churches related to each other in the New Testament (NT) which are examples for us to follow;*
4. *demonstrate that the NT did not identify any succession of church officers who had authority over more than one local church;*
5. *affirm that Scripture is totally sufficient so that which*

is not found in Scripture, either by precept or princi-
ple, should not be added on a pragmatic basis;

6. *show from Scripture and history that there is no basis*
for a hierarchy and that such a hierarchy is inconsis-
tent with Jesus' teaching on servant leadership;

7. *assert that the headship of Jesus Christ is a viable*
reality through the ministry of the Holy Spirit, thus
making a hierarchy unnecessary.

I will also attempt to demonstrate that the autonomy of
the local church is the only feasible way to practice the unity
of all Christians.

Probably all churches would claim to be a continuation
of the form and function of the New Testament Church, but
the only way one can be certain of this claim is to read the
New Testament and make the necessary comparisons. I will
endeavor to do just that. I would like to be as an artist who
helps people see more clearly what they are viewing.

I don't want to be presumptive, as though I had all the
answers, but I do want to help the readers focus on the NT
text. Thus, I hope every reader will find answers in the biblical text and not merely in my opinions.

The primary sections of this work have been submitted
to over 200 pastors of differing persuasions on this subject
who have read the critical portions and have made valuable
contributions. In a way, parts of this book are as much
theirs as mine; however, my space and your reading time do
not permit me to mention them all. To summarize, though,
the dominant observation made by these various pastors is
that the concept of the autonomy of the local church provides them the greatest freedom to serve the Lord according
to the dictates of their consciences.

Once I had the opportunity to attend a three-day spiritual-life seminar led by Armin Gesswine of the National Association of Evangelicals. He firmly taught that, "A biblical conviction about your local church is essential to revival." That seminar made an abiding impact on my life. It made me think more seriously, and profitably so, about the local church. This focus on the local church as defined by the NT made a difference in my life and I believe it can in yours. I am convinced that if churches would awaken to the NT teaching on the local church, it could be like the "awakening of a giant."

This was stated another way by Daryl Merrill where he uses Satan's imagined fears and words, quoting Leonard Ravenhill: "Let the church sleep! If she awakes, she will shake the world."[3] May God so rouse us to vital involvement!

Some don't have a clue what an "awakened church" looks like. Some have equated religious excitement with an awakening. Philip Yancey gives us a few challenging looks:

A friend of mine recently returned from a visit to Asian countries where Christians are experiencing persecution. Christians told him, *We're so blessed, because in Indonesia they're killing Christians, but here we just have to put up with discrimination and restrictions on our activities*.... Curious, I asked an old-time missionary, who had made a dozen trips to visit unregistered churches in China, if Christians there prayed for a change in restrictive government policies. He replied that not once had he heard a Chinese Christian pray for relief.... Last year, I visited Brazil... I met Brazilians who welcome homeless street urchins into their families, who bring food to prisoners voluntarily, not under anyone's organized program.

In the same article, he compares the situation in the US:

In the United States, nearly half attend church on a given Sunday, and Christians have a visible presence on university campuses and in every major profession.... Both church and parachurch seem to operate more like an industry than a living organism. We hire others to take care of the orphans and visit prisoners; we pay professionals to lead in worship. To return from a church in Brazil to one in the U.S. is like moving from a down-home country fair to one in the U.S. where everyone gets to pet the cows and chase the pigs, to Disney World's Animal Kingdom, where you pay a few dollars, mostly to watch beasts (some of which are mechanical) from behind a barrier.[4]

These and many other things cry out for a fresh awakening to a normal function and form of church life.

THE IMPORTANCE OF THIS SUBJECT

The importance of the Church is noted by Stanley Grenz, who says there has been a "lack of serious work in ecclesiology among evangelicals."[5] He addresses the lack of church involvement as culturally caused:

North American society is indeed imbued with individualism. The ethos of modern living orients itself toward the myth of the autonomous self.[6]

Unfortunately, we reflect our culture more than we affect it.

Life in the United States has become an intensely private affair. Most Americans are far more interested in being successful than in being faithful.[7]

And again from the same book:

Faith as the Bible describes it, however, is anything but a private affair. The New Testament portrays the Christian as a member of a family, a flock, a colony.[8]

Since Grenz' book, a number of significant books have been published, including: Kevin Giles', *What on Earth is the Church?* (Inter-Varsity Press); Edmund Clowney's, *The Church* (Inter-Varsity Press); and Craig Van Gelder's, *The Essence of the Church* (Baker Books). These needed writings show an awakening interest in this vital subject and have contributed valuable and scholarly insights into the understanding of church life. Craig Van Gelder's book strongly emphasizes the mission of the Church as an apostolic body, which I hope to keep in focus throughout this book.

Seemingly, though not actually, this contradicts Millard Erickson when he quotes John Macquarrie:

Probably more gets written on the Church nowadays than on any other single theological theme. Most of this writing, however, has been on a pragmatic basis. We hear about the Church in relation to rapid social change, the Church in a secular society, the Church and reunion, the Church in missions. However valuable some of the insights gained in these various fields may be, they need to be guided and correlated by a theological understanding of the Church.... At no point in the history of Christian thought has the doctrine of the Church received the direct and complete attention with other doctrines.... The new emphasis applying non-theological disciplines and methodologies to the study of the Church poses a danger as the Church struggles to understand itself theologically.[9]

Each of these authors and theologians recognizes the need for serious thought on the subject of the Church.

This book, unlike some to which I have referred, is written for the common reader and looks at the NT teaching on the Church from a congregational viewpoint. It sees each church as a local autonomous unit in the same way your family is a unit within itself. This form of the Church is as old as the earliest NT writings. It has been variously labeled "congregational," "independent," "dissenters," "local church," etc. Baptist churches, Churches of Christ, Plymouth Brethren, and others have sought to practice the autonomy of the local church (though some of these often do not take an inclusive approach).

Included are some chapters on the essential functions of the local church without which local churches lose their claim to being authentic. These chapters are needed because these functions reflect the true nature of the Church and they should not be determined merely by traditions or a hierarchy.

The practice of church life in the United States has been moving away from the traditional styles, such as are described by Clowney and Giles (referenced earlier). My purpose, however, is not to attack traditions, most of which have been practiced throughout Church history, but to show that they have not met the need nor corresponded altogether with Scripture and are not effectively reaching the world with the gospel.

Something different is happening today; *USA TODAY*[10] reports that the largest group of churches in the US is made up of non-denominational independent churches. In the article it was said that there are between 75,000 and 100,000 of this type in the US, as quoted by Lyle Schaller, an eminent interpreter of the sociology of the Church. These figures compared with 40,000 Southern Baptist churches and 20,000 Roman Catholic parishes.

Years ago I heard Donald Grey Barnhouse of Tenth Presbyterian in Philadelphia, Pennsylvania, say that there are only two forms of church government—one is exclusive and the other inclusive. As mentioned earlier, the scriptural pattern does not suggest that churches should be exclusive. One important advantage in the practice of the autonomous local church is that it can be inclusive as it sees one's church as a part of the family of churches throughout the world. Local churches can have mutual recognition, be inclusive, and cooperate in the proclamation of the gospel. I will develop this concept of inclusiveness in the chapter, "One in Christ."

THE NEW TESTAMENT CHURCH IN PRACTICE

The practice of Church life is the application of NT teachings to individuals and congregations. That there are missing ingredients in much that has been written on the subject of churches is evident in the lack of a transformational effect on the participants. To make certain this book sets forth a viable and practical approach that can be transforming (not just theologically correct), I have included chapters on the scriptural validity of membership and church attendance and the NT's teaching on the church service and on discipline.

It is my sincere desire that this book will make a practical difference in some small way to help that "awakening of a giant." It is plain that there is a need for "the church to be the

Church," particularly the church that you or I attend. A scripturally functioning church edifies people and equips them for works of service. I am hopeful, then, that the following pages will help some churches to be consistent with their name.

∾ Notes

1 Alston. *Guides to the Reformed Tradition.* 53.

2 All Scriptures are quoted from the New International Version (NIV) unless otherwise noted.

3 Merrill. *God's Order for the Local Church.* 2.

4 Yancey. *Christianity Today.* Feb. 5, 2001.

5 Grenz. *Revisioning Evangelical Theology.* 165.

6 Ibid. 149.

7 Shelley and Shelley. *The Consumer Church.* 51.

8 Ibid. 52.

9 Erickson. *Christian Theology.* 1027, 1026, and 1029 respectively.

10 *USA Today.* Jan. 27, 1997. 4.

CHAPTER ONE

THREE BASIC KINDS OF CHURCHES

Is it possible that it is this simple?

There are three basic forms of church government in the world. One is the episcopal system, the second is the presbyterian system, and the third is the local church system, often identified as independent or congregational (not the denomination bearing that name). Sometimes there is a mixture of these systems on a pragmatic rather than a scriptural basis, which complicates things. We call these systems of church government "church polity." These are self-descriptions used by the different church groups.

DEFINING DESIGNATIONS

❧ Episcopal

Episcopacy is church government by bishops who claim a lineal descent from the apostles appointed by the Lord Jesus. These bishops constitute a hierarchal form of government over both the lesser offices within the church and church members. Included are the Roman Catholic Church, the Episcopal Church, the Methodist Episcopal Church, the Orthodox churches, etc.

∽ Presbyterian

Presbyterianism (as worked out by John Calvin) is defined as this:

> Pastors and district Elders are comprised of one category of presbyters, of whom there were two divisions, one for teaching and the other for discipline.... [They performed their functions] "not by legal installation as in Roman Catholicism, but by virtue of the presence of the living Christ in the Spirit...." The ecclesiastical organization was not based by Calvin on the theory of the general priesthood of believers or on the right of the congregation to self-government, but simply on the need of discipline to prepare the way for the Word of God which, unlike civil justice, should influence the individual within.... [These officers were over districts, and] "independency was sharply opposed, and it was insisted that no regulation of an individual congregation could conflict with the general articles of the Church (Presbyterian)...." Discipline of pastors and Elders should be done by provincial synods.[1]

∽ Congregational

Congregationalism is the "gathered church principle," developed historically during the reign of Queen Elizabeth I (1558-1603).

> These became known as the 'Independents' or 'Dissenters'.... [They contended that] a church consisted of those who had personally responded to the call of Christ, and who had covenanted together with him and with one another to live together as his disciples.[2]

Leaders within this movement, which included some noteworthy scholars, demonstrated in their writings that this view of church life had roots that reached back to the first centuries of Christian history.

The local church system seeks to define itself by the primary mandate of the Lord Jesus in Matt. 16:17-19 and 18:15-20. These are the only recorded words of Jesus on the subject of the local church. It is the only system of church government able to recognize and include all churches built on the foundation of the gospel of Jesus Christ. This is true even though not all Christians are committed to this form of church government. This inclusiveness is a basis for the recognition and unity of true Christians. Other forms of church government are exclusive. These other forms of church organization are, in fact, organized divisions in the total company of Christians.

In this simplicity, churches are like families in the human race. Each family is a unit under God. No one is foolish enough to think that his or her family is the only family. So when a nation, such as Germany, claimed to be superior to all the rest, it was just a matter of time before this notion was discredited. There is an equality amongst Christians and churches. The family is a God-ordained unit, and all the social engineers have failed to improve on it. Of the family unit the Scriptures say:

Now I want you to realize that the head of every man is Christ, and the head of the woman is man, and the head of Christ is God (1 Cor. 11:3).

In the same way, the head of each spiritual family unit (local church) is Jesus Christ. He is in the midst, and he is able to communicate his headship through the Holy Spirit and the Scriptures.

Three institutions on earth are mandated by heaven, and these are the family, governments, and the local church. Each one is instituted by God, and our relationship to God affects our relationship to each one.

The Lord Jesus, in Matthew 16:18-19, said, *"And I tell you... Peter... on this rock I will build my church, and the gates of Hades will not overcome it."* These verses describe what has become known as the one universal mystical *invisible* "body of Christ," composed of all true Christians regardless of their religious affiliation. This understanding was first expressed in Church history by Clement, the earliest of the Church Fathers, and found clear expression in the writings of Augustine.

The *visible churches*, on the other hand, are the congregations described in over ninety references in the NT out of 114, in which believers find relationship, function, and responsibility. Of such, Earl Radmacher quotes Peter Fleming:

> A very important principle may be seen: the local church in its function and character stands in the same relation to Christ as the universal Church....[3]

❧ NOTES

[1] *The New Schaff-Herzog Religious Encyclopedia.* Vol. 9, 203.

[2] *The New Dictionary of Theology.* 159.

[3] Radmacher. *What the Church is all About.* 328.

CHAPTER TWO

BIBLICAL BASIS FOR THE LOCAL CHURCH

THE CHARTER FOR THE FORM AND FUNCTION OF THE LOCAL CHURCH

Three institutions on earth are chartered by heaven and one of them is your church. The Scriptures are the terms of that charter.

What do I mean by a charter? *Random House Dictionary* defines it as:

> ...a document, issued by a sovereign... outlining the conditions under which [in this instance] a body is organized, and defining its rights and privileges.

The Lord Jesus chartered local churches in Matthew 18:15-18. This is the charter of local churches since it is one of two passages where Jesus uses the word "church," and this is the only one that mentions a local assembly and includes a description of a church's operation while the first one, in Matthew 16:18, describes the totality of all true believers. The common use throughout the New Testament, however, refers to a local congregation in over ninety of the 114 times it occurs.

Consider this list of fundamental principles regarding a local church found in Matthew 18:

1. It is a redemptive and restorative community.

It is evident from the context of the passage of Scripture in Matthew 18 that churches are redemptive and restorative institutions reflecting the character of their Lord. The chapter opens with a lesson on humility, places great worth on a little child, and then extends this to the significance of a single sheep. The restoration of the wandering sheep leads right into the fold of a local church. Remember, this is in the context of our Lord's one and only recorded statement about a local church. The section immediately following this "charter of a local church" is Jesus' most powerful teaching on forgiveness (18:21-35). Therefore, it is most reasonable to understand a local church as a society of forgiven and forgiving people brought into the fold.

2. It is the family of Christ in a given location.

Jesus identified the relationships of those within the local church as brothers: *"If a brother..."* (Matt. 18:15). A "brother" is defined by Jesus' words, *"My mother and brothers are those who hear God's word and put it into practice"* (Luke 8:21). In our common usage it describes a born-again person, a child of God. This means that the church is a *regenerate* body of people. As he instituted families for the natural world, so Jesus instituted spiritual families and established the principles governing family life for redeemed people in church families. From the context of Jesus' words in this chapter, we are instructed as to our mutual responsibilities. We *are* our brother's keepers.

3. It is a disciplined family.

We are directed to act in concert with others: *"take one or two others along..."* (18:16). There is a responsibility to listen to one another: *"if he will not listen"* (18:16) and *"If he refuses to listen..."* (18:17). Individualism gives way to corporate life. The church family is a disciplined family where the members' relationships to each other are mediated by Jesus' words. Brothers are responsible for and accountable to one another, and discipline is carried out, not by a hierarchal person but by one another. These lines underscore the importance of the relationships within this family as well as the holy character of this gathering.

4. It is a gathered church—the family gathers together.

The idea of a gathered company or an "assembly" is inherent in Jesus' usage of the word "church." The head of the family gathers with his family. The gathering is in the name of the Lord. *"For where two or three come together in my name..."* (18:20). Attendance is implicit. It doesn't even require ten families as it did to form a synagogue. His *NAME* is placed on the gathering. It reminds us of how Jehovah placed his *NAME* in a specific place in the Old Testament (OT) (Deut. 12:5).

The size of the gathering need not be large: *"For where two or three come together..."* (18:20). Further, religious organizations which claim to be the one and only true church and, therefore, imply that a congregation must gather in their denominational name to be legitimate are contradicted by this passage. The name of Jesus and his presence are certainly sufficient to make a gathering authentic.

5. It is the family's final court of appeal.

The local congregation is the final court of appeal, and it is the "supreme court" for believers: *"If he refuses to listen to them, tell it to the church; and if he refuses to listen even to the church, treat him as a pagan..."* (18:17). There is no higher court to which one might appeal, according to the Lord Jesus. This *excludes any form of ecclesiastical hierarchy.*

6. This body has power to "bind" and "loose."

"I tell you the truth, whatever you bind on earth will be bound in heaven..." (18:18). It doesn't take ten or a thousand churches to exercise this power granted to a local church. A local church with Jesus amongst them is adequate for the task he assigns.

7. It is a defined company.

The people in this description of a church were defined as a family of "brothers," and those outside were to be treated as "pagans." Clearly, a person was a regenerate "brother" and belonged to "the church" or they were not a part of the church. Formal or informal, there is a form of membership. This makes a case for a visibly identified group of people and excludes the concept of an "invisible church." One person said, "If we don't quit preaching about the 'invisible' church, it will become that way." When reconciliation fails within the family, the disciplined person is publicly disciplined: *"tell it to the church"* (18:17). It is evident that the task of telling it to the church requires a local church. If it is the "invisible" church, whom do you tell? If it is the collection of churches in a geographical area, consider the logistical problems one would have had before modern forms of communication existed.

8. The family primarily functions by agreement.

The family relates to its head, and does so by means of prayer. The family is joined in prayer. *"Again, I tell you that if two of you on earth agree about anything you ask for, it will be done for you by my Father in heaven"* (18:19). It is a local fulfillment of Jesus' words in Mark 11:27 as quoted from Isa. 56:7: *"My house will be called a house of prayer for all nations."*

THE HEAD OF THE FAMILY IS IN THE MIDST OF THE FAMILY GATHERING.

In this overall picture, we must remember that the Lord is the owner (Acts 20:28). It is his church. He must be consulted about everything we do. We are his stewards. This needs application as to how we act and even how we deal with material things, how we relate to a pastor, how we discipline a person, etc. To be in agreement with others but to fail to be in agreement with the Lord makes all we do meaningless.

Nothing should come between the body and its head, between the shepherd and his sheep, or between the heavenly Bridegroom and his bride.

Again, it is his Church. He called it together with his own voice in the gospel. He called it unto himself. Each one who is a member has been personally called. This makes the Church authentic. It isn't just a clone of a certain kind of church. It has an identity all of its own. The Lord calls this Church to a particular mission.

Of Jesus' words, *"For where two or three come together in my name, there I am with them"* (Matt. 18:20), Clifford Christensen, Conference Minister of the Conservative Congregational Conference, has said, "This is the most important truth in the understanding of congregational polity." Christ's personal presence alters everything anyone can say about church government or polity. The "head" of the Church is in the midst! All is done by his authority. He is central to all activity. He is the one to be pleased. He is the resource for the local church so it can rise above all of its natural limitations. He is the sufficiency of the local body. He is the head, and the "headquarters" is where the head is. He is, in fact, the Lord of each local church.

There is no need to bypass him to look for oversight and guidance. This is evident in the words of the Spirit from the Lord in his message to the seven churches of Asia (Rev. 2 and 3). He who was dead and is now alive, who possesses the keys of death and hell, speaks to the angels of these churches. He was "among the lampstands" (Rev. 1:13). They are not the "church in Asia" but the "seven church-es." Jesus is their only hierarchy. No church was over the others. They were all sister churches directly under their Lord and joined to one another through him.

SOME ESSENTIALS WE NEED TO CONSIDER

We have been looking specifically at the facts regarding a local church as described in Matthew 18. Now let us also consider some additional scriptural guidelines and parame-ters in the following areas:

1. "Authority" is the key word when speaking of church polity.

Since we are talking about church government, or church polity, if you will, the essential word is "authority."

From whom or from where do we get authority to do what we do? From whom do we get our rights? In our democratic society, we think we get our rights from the votes of our congregations. But if our voting is other than a collective way of expressing what we prayerfully perceive is the Lord's will, it is a usurpation of authority. The purpose of our business meetings must be a prayerful seeking of the will of our Lord.

Certainly, our authority is not derived from a hierarchal figure in some other place but from him who is the "head." I can remember a brief time in my life when I was the head of a tiny church organization. I received a letter from a national pastor on the mission field asking me what to do with some mission property. I pondered the problems involved. I went out for a prayer walk. The more I prayed and the more I thought about the Scripture, the more I realized that God had not given me any authority over the property in a distant land. When I returned to my office, I simply sat down and wrote the national pastor a letter, telling him to assemble the relevant congregation together and prayerfully make a decision. That incident became an important part of my pilgrimage into a congregational way of life.

Here is another learning experience in my life: I sat and listened to the head of a Bible college dialogue with the moderator of a national organization. The college head, arguing for an autonomous local church, asked the moderator, "In that you are the head of your denomination, to whom do you look for supervision, or to whom do you submit yourself and your church?"

To this the moderator answered, "I, with the leadership in my congregation, make our decisions."

The Bible college head replied, "I am only asking that all churches use the same model as you use." It doesn't take much thought to realize that other heads of organizations do the same thing. If they can prayerfully do so, after mutual consultation with their leaders, may we not use the same model for our local churches? Cannot the Lord, the ultimate authority, give us the directions for which we so often look to others? Or are we to think he is unable to speak?

2. Practice of local autonomy is consistent in the NT.

There is a pattern for the function of the local church.

They devoted themselves to the apostles' teaching and to the fellowship, to the breaking of bread and to prayer.... And the Lord added to their number daily those who were being saved (Acts 2:42,47).

As Moses saw the pattern of the tabernacle when he was on Mount Sinai, so we see the pattern in the New Testament.

"Scripture does not take the form of credal and doctrinal statements, although these are unquestionably woven within its structure," writes Alistair McGrath. Doctrinal markers usually arise out of conflict. Hence, we are not surprised when we don't find the explicit definitive doctrinal statements some would wish; rather, we find picture, pattern, and precedence.[1]

3. The significance of precedence or pattern.

Look at a lawyer's library to see the significance of precedence, or look at an architect's drawings to see the importance of a drawing/picture or model. Remember the saying, "A picture is worth ten thousand words." In law, it determines a decision. For the builder, it guides him. For the communicator, it turns abstract concepts into a visual reality. It is what God showed Moses on the mount; it is what we see in the New Testament.

Hence, it seems rather precarious when people give little weight to the "pictures" we find in Scripture when deciding if there is a biblical and non-biblical way to do church.

With this in mind, consider the word-picture in Revelation of the lampstands as a pattern. Consider the precedence when we find separate churches in the city of Rome (Rom. 16:16) and Paul's respect for the local authority of the church at Corinth (2 Cor. 2:10).

These and other passages support that which is implicit in Jesus' words, *"...if he refuses to listen to the church* [plainly a local congregation], *treat him as a pagan"* (Matt. 18:18-20).

According to Paul Minear, biblical scholar, "...there are no less than ninety-six pictures of the church in the pages of the New Testament alone."[2]

The principles identified in the charter of Matthew 18 are consistently practiced throughout the NT. Let's look at two noteworthy examples: First, when there was a conflict between Antioch's missionary representatives, Barnabas and Paul, those who went out from Jerusalem met with them as equal representatives of the two churches, not as one over the other, as they ironed out their differences (Acts 15). It was not a "general council" but a meeting of two sister churches.

The second example is quite different but very instructive. When Paul wrote to the Corinthian church about forgiving a repentant man, *"If you forgive anyone, I also forgive him"* (2 Cor. 2:10), he showed respect for the disciplinary authority of that local body after the pattern of Matthew 18. And even though he was the apostle to the Gentiles, he did not exert authority over the function of an established assembly by doing the hierarchal thing. In fact, he said, *"Not that we lord it over you, but we work with you for your joy"* (2 Cor. 1:24).

4. Our local church is God's temple.

Don't you know that you [Gk. plural] yourselves are God's temple and that God's Spirit lives in you? If anyone destroys God's temple, God will destroy him; for God's temple is sacred, and you are that temple (1 Cor. 3:16,17).

This astounding declaration lifts a church's sense of identity above all other human institutions, just as the "temple" lifted the meaning of the Jewish temple above all other religious temples in the world in the Old Testament. It gives the Church a realization of God's presence, a perception greatly needed in our time.

To appreciate the significance of these words, one needs only to read the things said about the temple of the Lord in the Old and New Testaments. They are awesome indeed. In the NT we see that people are *"built together to become a dwelling in which God lives by his Spirit"* (Eph. 2:22). The situation at Corinth that provoked the declaration in 1 Corinthians 3 was the way in which the Corinthians were becoming followers of Paul, Peter, and Apollos instead of Christ. We need to be more careful when we say we "belong" to this or that denomination, thus repeating the divisive error of the Corinthians. Paul's declaration altered our perception of the nature of the Church and distinguished it from human institutions. It is God's temple.

5. The Holy Spirit, the Regent of Jesus Christ.

Jesus sent the Holy Spirit in his place (John 16:5,7,15). Therefore, the "regent of Christ" is the Holy Spirit and not some ecclesiastical personage. A "regent" is a person who exercises ruling power in the absence of a sovereign. Some ecclesiastical leaders usurp the ministry of the Holy Spirit. The Church is his temple, his domain. *And in him you too are being built together to become a dwelling in which God lives by his Spirit"* (Eph. 2:22). He is present, he sees, he hears, he speaks, and he makes the headship of Jesus Christ a viable reality. When Ananias and Sapphira lied to the church, they lied to the Holy Spirit: (Acts 5:9). *"The Spirit told Philip…"* (Acts 8:29); *"…the Spirit said to him, 'Simon, three men are looking for you…'"* (Acts 10:19); he sends forth workers into the harvest field (Acts 13:2,3); he restrains and redirects the Lord's missionaries (Acts 16:6-10); he delegates and exercises ecclesiastical authority (Acts 20:20). In all, he superintends, guides, gifts, and administrates.

Before leaving this subject, let me carefully distance myself from what I now see as the "cult of the Spirit," which operates as if one had a hotline to heaven, and does not subject itself to the written Word of God. The Spirit and the Word must agree. They are as Siamese twins—one doesn't appear without the other. Without this qualification, we could be hopelessly at sea.

6. Our local church is called "the body of Christ."

"Now you are the body of Christ, and each one of you is a part of it" (1 Cor. 12:27). When we hear this title, we tend only to think of the invisible mystical body of Christ (Eph. 4:4). But when Paul uses this analogy in Corinthians, he does so to visualize the church at Corinth. The "hands," "eyes," and "feet" were each individually a part of that church. The Holy Spirit had baptized them into the functional "body of Christ" by which the indwelling presence of the Spirit would

make Christ visible, just as your body makes you visible. The "gifts of the Spirit" are the abilities of Christ manifested by his body. When one grasps that Paul is likening the parts of the "body" to the gifts of the Spirit, one is compelled to accept the fact that those gifts are for today. Christ does not have a dysfunctional body. When we understand that the local church is "the body of Christ" indwelt by him, our whole concept of our church is altered and our expectations raised, and we are careful what we attach to Jesus' body.

7. Our local church is a covenant community.

Our local church is a covenant family, witnessed to by the fact that we have a Communion service. In that service we often read the words of our Lord, *"This is my blood of the covenant, which is poured out for many for the forgiveness of sins"* (Matt. 26:28). This demonstrates the continuity between the Passover of the Old Testament and the Communion service. (I believe that the Exodus is the primary literary motif behind the New Testament.)

Alfred Edersheim said that the Passover and the Feast of Unleavened Bread underlies "the whole history of Israel."[3] It commemorated the first time Israel "became a people" and its celebration repeatedly confirmed Israel's covenant relationship to Jehovah. So when the Lord Jesus, in fulfillment of Jeremiah 31:31, said that his blood was the "blood of the new covenant," he clearly indicated this continuity as well as the covenant membership of the communicants.

In the Old Testament the Passover was celebrated in two places, in the temple and in the Jewish home. Jesus' inauguration of Communion was a "family" situation, and the local church was to perpetuate that family situation. The redeemed were placed in families.

38

The regulations as to who could participate in the Passover celebration are reflected in passages dealing with church discipline: *"Therefore let us keep the Festival, not with the old yeast..."* (1 Cor. 5:8). In this case there is the issue of the sin of leaven/yeast which correlates with the Jewish practice of removing all leaven from their homes in preparation for the Passover celebration.

Though there is not space here to present and explain the many NT passages that tie into this theme, yet it is plain that the local church celebrates the fact that it is a "covenant family" under obligation to discipline according to the covenant and to possess the authority derived from the covenant.

8. What about apostolic succession?

One may ask, "Did not the apostles fulfill this function, and did they not appoint successors to take their place and form a hierarchal administration on earth?" Though the apostles were Christ's special appointed delegates, they did not appoint persons to succeed themselves. Thus we see the twelve *"apostles of the lamb"* as the foundation of the New Jerusalem (Rev. 21:14). One only needs to read the farewell letters of the apostles Paul and Peter to see that they taught an apostolic succession of *truth* but not of persons. There is no mention of their successors, but Paul did say:

And the things you have heard me say in the presence of many witnesses entrust to reliable men who will also be qualified to teach others (2 Tim. 2:2).

These reliable men were the elders of the church, and through their ministry the church was to be the *"pillar and foundation of the truth"* (1 Tim. 3:15). These elders succeeded the apostle Paul.

If we teach that there are apostles today on the same level as the Twelve, this opens up the canon of Scripture to new additions and it fundamentally alters what we believe and practice with regard to church government. Not many would be willing to receive the following words from someone claiming to be an apostle today: *"If anybody thinks he is a prophet or spiritually gifted, let him acknowledge that what I am writing is the Lord's command"* (1 Cor. 14:17). Would you be willing to obey some reputed "apostle" or "prophet" who said, *"If anyone does not obey our instruction in this letter... Do not associate with him, in order that he may feel ashamed"* (2 Thess. 3:14)?

We recognize that the twelve apostles have a special relationship to God's program on earth and, through their witness and teaching, they became the foundation of the Church (Rev. 21:14). In a special sense we have the Twelve with us in our churches when we have the Scriptures. "Accordingly, the local church... is the seat of authority in the Church of Christ."[4] Each church was directly responsible to use the Scriptures as their authoritative guide.

∿ NOTES

[1] McGrath. *The Genesis of Doctrine.*

[2] Shelley and Shelley. *The Consumer Church.* 48.

[3] Edersheim. *The Temple—Its Ministry and Services.* 209.

[4] *Lutheran Cyclopedia.* 824, 825.

CHAPTER THREE

THE FOUNDATION OF GOD'S HOUSE

*The foundation determines the form of a structure,
and the form is designed for its function.*

I will endeavor to show that the various passages mentioning the "foundation" can be harmonized to express one basic concept of the foundation.

The foundation unites that which is built upon it and it is one with the building. This chapter will show the oneness of the diverse descriptions of what the New Testament describes as the foundation for faith and practice.

THE FOUNDATION

*...you are no longer foreigners and aliens, but fellow
citizens with God's people and members of God's
household, built on the foundation of the apostles and
prophets, with Christ Jesus himself as the chief corner-
stone* (Eph. 2:19,20).

The foundation of the Church is the Word of God given to us by the apostles and prophets.

SOLA SCRIPTURA

"Sola Scriptura" is the Latin phrase used by the leaders of the Reformation as they called Christianity back to its foundation. It meant that the Scriptures alone were the ultimate authority for faith and practice. This resulted in a biblical revival of faith and experience that impacted the entire Christian world. The Scriptures bear witness to their sufficiency:

All Scripture is God-breathed and is useful for teaching, rebuking, correcting and training in righteousness, so that the man of God may be thoroughly equipped for every good work (2 Tim. 3:16,17).

Thomas Oden said:

This is why we study Scripture—not pile up more data regarding the cultural determinants of religion.... Whatever the renewal of the church requires is furnished to us through Scripture.[1]

Since the time of the Reformation some have sought to alter the position of Sola Scriptura by adding tradition, the Church, and experience. Time has shown that these additions dilute the restoring power of Scripture.

On this subject, Donald G. Bloesch notes that, "For the most part both the patristic fathers and the medieval theologians before the fourteenth century taught that the Bible is the unique and sole source of revelation." Bloesch continues, "The priority of Scripture over traditions was clearly enunciated by Thomas Aquinas [major Roman Catholic theologian].... Arguments from Scripture are used properly and carry necessity in matters of faith; arguments from other

42

doctors of the Church are proper, but carry only probability; for our faith is based on the revelation given to the apostles and prophets who wrote the canonical books of the Scriptures and not on revelations that could have been made to other doctors."[2]

The Holy Spirit turns the Bible into a "talking book," wherein we hear the voice of God speaking to our hearts. In the words of Os Guinness:

Words are the deepest, fullest expression in which God now discloses himself to us. So it is in listening to him, trusting him and obeying him when he calls that we 'let God be God' in all of his awe and majesty.[3]

There is a strong attempt to unite tradition with Scripture, as evident in the Protestant and Catholic agreements now being written and re-written. Unfortunately, in my mind, this attempt includes many outstanding evangelicals whom we never expected to participate in such an effort. In pursuit of healing the breach of the Reformation, many are saying that tradition is equal to Scripture. Professor Olson of Bethel College and Seminary, in the letters to the editor in *Christianity Today*,[4] writes:

I fear we are in danger of falling into the error of two equal sources of absolute authority—Scripture and tradition.

THE CHURCH MUST BE BUILT ON
THE CLOSED CANON.

The Church is built upon the revelation of Jesus Christ given to the apostles and prophets. That revelation, written under the inspiration of the Holy Spirit, is our Bible. Jesus predicted its completion when he predicted that the Spirit would *"guide you into all truth"* (John 16:13). So, when they were so guided they wrote it down for us. This prediction to "guide you into all truth" was limited to those who were with Jesus *"from the beginning"* (John 15:27) and could not include others who would seek to add their "revelations" to Scripture at some later time.

John gave us some objective criteria: *"Every spirit that acknowledges that Jesus Christ is come in the flesh is from God..."* and, *"We are from God, and whoever knows God listens to us.... This is how we recognize the Spirit of truth and the spirit of falsehood"* (1 John 4:2,6). People often quote the first and omit the second. And who the "us" is in this passage is made clear in the first verse of the first chapter of the same letter:

> *That which was from the beginning, which we have heard, which we have seen with our eyes, which we have looked at and our hands have touched—this we proclaim concerning the Word of life* (1 John 1:1).

Certainly, these words limit the explanation of "who" to those who had been with Jesus from the beginning (John 15:27) and exclude modern "apostles" who would add their "revelations" to Scripture.

If we don't affirm a completed canon, we open the door to evolution of truth, such as is found in most cults. The word *canon* means "a rule of measure." By the Scriptures we measure all preaching and practices. Our measure must not be made of elastic. (Can you imagine someone measuring with an elastic yard stick? That seems to be what is happening in our times.) No tradition, reasoning, experience, church council, or "revelation" can be added to Scripture as a foundation upon which the Church is to build. We need the illumination of the Spirit on the Scripture but we don't need any added revelations. History, through the various church councils, has contributed a valued commentary on Scripture but has not added to Scripture. Therefore, we follow the dictum of the Reformation: "Where the Bible speaks we speak and where the Bible is silent we are silent."

When people add to this foundation, they end up building a lean-to on God's house. As I expect others to be measured by Scripture, so I urge the reader to measure what I am saying by the same canon of Scripture.

JESUS IS THE FOUNDATION OF THE CHURCH REVEALED IN SCRIPTURE.

When Jesus said, in Matt. 16:18, *"I will build my church,"* he also said that it would be upon *"this rock,"* which referred to Peter's confession, *"You are the Christ, the Son of the living God"* (Matt. 16:16). Christ alone is "rock-solid," the One on whom you can always depend, *"the same yesterday and today and forever"* (Heb. 13:8). This is consistent with the rest of Scripture which tells us that the Lord is our rock. It agrees with Peter's and Paul's statements about the "rock." Peter could not be the rock for he wasn't sufficiently "rock-like" (Gal. 2:11-14), and his ministry was specifically to the Jews (Gal. 2:7).

> *So then, no more boasting about men! All things are yours, whether Paul or Apollos or Cephas* [Peter] *or the world or life or death or the present or the future— all are yours, and you are of Christ, and Christ is of God* (1 Cor. 3:21-23).

THE FOUNDATION IS THE GOSPEL CONCERNING JESUS CHRIST.

There are over eighty references to the gospel in the epistles. It is the message of the "voice" of the Good Shepherd which his sheep hear. It is the *"power of God for the salvation of everyone who believes"* (Rom. 1:16).

> *Now to him who is able to establish you* ["bring into being on a firm or permanent basis"5] *by my gospel and the proclamation of Jesus Christ, according to the revelation of the mystery hidden for long ages past, but now revealed and made known through the prophetic writings by the command of the eternal God, so that all nations might believe and obey him—to the only wise God, be glory forever through Jesus Christ! Amen* (Rom. 16:25-27).

This gospel-foundation of the Church and of Christ's churches is that which supports the unity of Christians.

THIS GOSPEL OF JESUS CHRIST IS ABOUT THE CHRIST EVENT.

The gospel is not a philosophy or a set of ethics. It is the gospel of a Person. It is about the coming of Christ in time and space, the time when the Son of God became a man that he might die in our stead and rise again, the righteous for the unrighteous. The Old Testament predicted this event, the Gospels are the historical record of this event, the Epistles explain the meaning and significance of this event, and the Revelation unfolds the ultimate effect of the Christ event.

> *For what I received, I passed on to you as of first importance: that Christ died for our sins according to the*

Scriptures, that he was buried, that he was raised the third day according to the Scriptures (1 Cor. 15:3,4).

This is the one and only gospel upon which we rest our faith and upon which our churches rest. *"For I resolved to know nothing while I was with you except Jesus Christ and him crucified"* (1 Cor. 2:2).

For he has set a day when he will judge the world with justice by the man he has appointed. He has given proof of all this to all men by raising him from the dead (Acts 17:31).

This will take place on the day when God will judge men's secrets through Jesus Christ, as my gospel declares (Rom. 2:16).

THE PROCLAMATION OF THE CHRIST EVENT IS GOD'S CALL.

The Church is God's called-out company of people, called together by the proclamation of the gospel. *Ekklesia,* which is translated "church," means "called out." Included in the meaning of the word is "assembly" or "gathering." Hence, everyone who heard the gospel in faith was saved and *"added to their number"* (Acts 2:47) and built on the foundation. People who hear and respond to Christ gather to him and with Christ's people. *"For where two or three come together in my name, there am I with them"* (Matt. 18:20).

R. C. Trench explains that, "*Ekklesia* is a secular word that was consecrated with a deeper meaning in the Christian world."[6] Further:

It described a lawful assembly in a free Greek city of all those possessed of the rights of citizenship for the transaction of public affairs.[7]

Though the word was in regular use in the secular world, it never was used with the definite article, but is consistently so used in the NT. Kicklightner said:

> The lack of the definite article in the classical writings indicates that something about the essential nature of the religious *ekklesia* found no analogy in the secular *ekklesia*.... It remains, then, to determine if the word *ekklesia* received a religious meaning or connotation in the Septuagint.[8]

The Septuagint (the Greek translation of the Old Testament in use when the New Testament was written) often translates the Hebrew *qahal* with *ekklesia*. Of *qahal*, Radmacher says:

> ...*qahal* comes from the same root as *qol*, the word for "voice," suggests that the Old Testament *qahal* was the community summoned by the Divine Voice, by the Word of God. It was the people who heard God's voice in the Word of God.[9]

THIS PROCLAMATION IS THE "FOUNDATION" FOR A LOCAL CHURCH.

> *By the grace God has given me, I laid a foundation as an expert builder.... For no one can lay any foundation other than the one already laid, which is Jesus Christ* (1 Cor. 3:10,11).

Each believer is built on the foundation of this gospel. *"By this gospel you are saved..."* (1 Cor. 15:2). Even as a natural foundation determines the form of that which is built upon it, so the gospel-foundation determines the form of the NT congregation. All must be consistent with the gospel.

THIS MAKES IT POSSIBLE FOR US TO RECOGNIZE TRUE CHURCHES.

Faith in the true gospel *unites* Christians and overrides the man-made divisions that divide God's larger family. Our oneness is in the gospel concerning Christ and not in any form of church government, particular doctrinal emphasis, or style of worship. This excludes one from taking the principles of the autonomous church and applying them in a sectarian way, refusing to recognize the many denominations preaching the gospel. The gospel is far greater than those things about which Christians differ. It is not a matter of being Baptist, Presbyterian, Episcopalian, etc. The uniting issue is faith in the gospel. It is a sin against the gospel to magnify our differences and thus to reject those who believe the gospel. This gospel is not to be confused with our responses to it. It is about what God has done and not about what we are supposed to do.

> *For Christ did not send me to baptize, but to preach the gospel—not with words of human wisdom, lest the cross of Christ be emptied of its power* (1 Cor. 1:17).

Much of the transforming power of the gospel is lacking today because many things have been *added* to the gospel of God's grace.

> *We proclaim to you what we have seen and heard, so that you also may have fellowship with us. And our fellowship is with the Father and with his Son, Jesus Christ* (1 John 1:3).

THE CHURCH IS "THE PILLAR AND FOUNDATION OF THE TRUTH" (1 Tim. 3:15).

Amazingly, in the same breath in which Paul says the (local) church is the house of God and pillar and ground of truth, he says:

> He [Jesus] *appeared in a body, was vindicated by the Spirit, was seen by angels, was preached among the nations, was believed on in the world, was taken up in glory* (1 Tim. 3:16).

Churches and the Christ event are joined. The truths about the Lord Jesus and the NT Church are inseparable. The Church is built upon that truth and becomes one with the truth upon which it is built. The truth is the very nature of the Church. It becomes as solid as that upon which it is built: *"...the gates of Hades will not overcome it"* (Matt. 16:18). People *"born again, not of perishable seed, but of imperishable, through the living and enduring word of God"* (1 Pet. 1:23) are themselves called *"living stones... built into a spiritual house"* (1 Pet. 2:5) *"built together to become a dwelling in which God lives by his Spirit"* (Eph. 2:22). *"To him be glory in the church and in Christ Jesus throughout all generations, for ever and ever! Amen"* (Eph. 3:21). Hence, there is nothing temporary about God's Church.

This Church is about truth, and it is a travesty when we become an institution built upon a personality, a program, a worship style, a psychological support group, etc. The Church is God's depository of truth. The local church is:

> ...the principal outward means to support, preserve, publish, declare, and propagate the doctrine or truth

of the gospel, especially concerning the person and offices of Christ ...."[10]

When conditions are dreadful around us, we are exhorted to *"Preach the Word..."* (2 Tim. 4:2). We are not to become as convenience stores dispensing hot dogs and candy bars and gasoline. Our product is the truth! Package it however you will but make certain the package has the full weight of truth in it. Don't let the packaging outweigh the truth. Let us remember that what we win people with is what we win them to.

Serious thought as to what the Scriptures teach about God and his relationship to his universe is called theology. That part of theology which treats the Church is called *ecclesiology*—its form and function. In ecclesiology we dare not trivialize what God has said in his Word about church matters.

> Theological emptiness undermines and eventually destroys the most gifted servants.... A theology driven ministry focuses on real needs, not on felt needs.[11]

The same periodical quotes J. I. Packer as saying, "Spiritual life is fostered, and spiritual maturity engendered, not by techniques but by truth."

Someone has described some of what is being dispensed in these days of "touchy-feely" religion as being not much more than "tea-leaf psychiatry."

It is said that there has been a movement from theology to methodology. This was reiterated when I heard a seminary president say that the seminary's emphasis would now shift from theology to methodology, particularly focusing on the administration and growth of churches. This raises the question as to what the apostle Paul meant when he wrote, *"For the time will come when men will not put up with sound doctrine"* (2 Tim. 4:3).

At the same time, I don't want to make a case for intolerance and the un-Christian way that people divided the Christian community with an overemphasis on this or that doctrine. (As I see it, heresy may be just a divisive overemphasis of a particular doctrine.)

We are in need of making our churches God-centered, where we fit the description of a *"pillar and foundation of truth"* (1 Tim. 3:15) instead of man-centered therapy centers.

WHAT IS TRUTH?

Jesus said, *"I am… the truth…"* (John 14:6). He is the one *"in whom are hidden all the treasures of wisdom and knowledge"* (Col. 2:3). *"Sanctify them by the truth; your word is truth"* (John 17:17). Truth is constant and universal. Some, in trying to be contemporary, indulge novel fads and lose all sense of biblical or historical theology, even including a changing God (process theology). Some "truths" being proclaimed today don't meet the definition of truth. Some of what is being taught in the US is totally inapplicable in the Third World. Emotional excitement not produced by proclaiming God's Word needs to be abandoned. At times we mirror our culture far more than we bear witness to timeless and universal truths.

The plain truth of Scripture must not be obscured by deeper meanings, coded messages, or allegorical or "spiritualized" interpretations. Granted, there are passages that are difficult to understand, but these must be interpreted by those which are plain in their meanings. Poor or bad hermeneutics can destroy the biblical foundation upon which the Church is built. The Bible becomes a self-interpreting book when we compare Scripture with Scripture. We need neither pope nor guru to tell us the authoritative meaning. We need to humbly and prayerfully read the Scripture, comparing Scripture with Scripture. Then we will know the Bible is God's talking book in which we hear his voice. The Holy Spirit will illuminate its pages and thoroughly equip us *for every good work* (2 Tim. 3:17).

To sum this up, let me illustrate: An admiral, while commanding a battleship cruising on a foggy night off the coast, directed his signalman to signal to what he thought was a destroyer, directing it to yield the right-of-way to his oncoming battleship. The reply came back that the admiral would have to change his course. The infuriated admiral immediately replied through his signalman, "I am an admiral and this is a battleship. Your destroyer must yield the right-of-way." This time the reply came back, "You will have to change your course because this is a lighthouse and not a ship, and I am on land." That dramatically demonstrates the point because the Word of God is a fixed lighthouse as a guide to us all, and those who ignore the eternal truths therein will most certainly end up in shipwreck even though they may be intellectual "admirals."

WE MUST APPLY SOLA SCRIPTURA TO CHURCH GOVERNMENT.

Many believe that the Scriptures are silent on this subject and, therefore, they are free to do what they think works best. This seems to be an avoidance of what is plain. It doesn't follow the dictum, "Where the Scriptures are silent, we are silent." It presumes that the God who was meticulously definitive in his plans for the tabernacle/temple left us to our imagination for the organization of his Church and churches. This ignores about a hundred specific passages concerning local churches in the NT. It then chooses to add to these Scriptures ideas drawn from the surrounding culture. The criteria then becomes just what seems to work best.

Misnamed Bible conferences are, at times, preoccupied with "what works" and little with the teaching of Scripture. This has changed the simplicity of the NT Church into a variety of complex organizations, most of which are schismatic. This, in turn, builds walls between fellow Christians. Such complexity makes recognition of our fellow Christians almost impossible. It has been a movement from inclusiveness to exclusiveness.

In the following chapters I hope to show the simplicity of the NT churches, using the precepts, principles, and patterns that abound throughout the NT. Consider the following quotes from John Owen:

> ...the Lord is our judge, the Lord is our statute-maker, the Lord is our king... men, under what pretense or name [have no] right or authority to constitute any new frame or order of the church, to make any laws of their own for its rule or government.... If men had not been weary of apostolical simplicity and humility, if they could have contented themselves with the honour and dignity annexed unto their office and work by Christ himself, if they had never entertained pleasing dreams of thrones, preeminencies, chief sees, secular grandeur and power, nor framed so many laws and canons about these things....[12]

One is reminded of a famous quote from Martin Luther:

> I ask for the Scriptures and Eck offers me the Fathers.

I ask for the sun, and he shows me his lanterns. I ask where is your Scripture proof? and he adduces Ambrose and Cyril.... With all due respect to the Fathers, I prefer the authority of Scripture.[13]

In conclusion, it is not difficult to see the agreement of the passages of Scripture about the foundation and how they complete and complement each other. The foundation of the great mystical invisible Church is the same as the foundation of each local church.

Therefore, if I fail to build on the foundation of Scripture, correct me but don't ignore me.

∿ NOTES

[1] Oden. *Bible Commentary, 1 and 2 Timothy.* 26.

[2] Geisler and McKenzie. *Roman Catholics and Evangelicals.*

[3] Guinness. *The Call.*

[4] *Christianity Today.* April 6, 1998.

[5] *Random House Dictionary.*

[6] Trench. *Synonyms of the New Testament.*

[7] *Liddell and Scott's Greek Lexicon.*

[8] Radmacher. *What the Church is all About.* 121.

[9] Ibid. 126.

[10] Dr. James Means, Assoc. Prof. of Pastoral Ministry at Denver Seminary in *Focal Point.*

[11] Op. cit.

[12] Owen. *The Works of John Owen.* Vol. 15, pp. 228, 239, 241.

[13] Farrar, *The History of Interpretation.* 327.

CHAPTER FOUR

ONE IN CHRIST

*Is the ecumenical movement the answer? Should we
return to Rome? Is a super organization what we
need? How are we going to answer questions
about divisions in the Church?*

The form of a New Testament church is such that it fits
with other churches to express oneness in Christ.

Our oneness in Christ is the basis for unity among all
true Christians, and the autonomous definition of a local
church is the only structural definition that can include all
other forms of church polity. Attempts to organize that
unity into an association, a super-church, or a denomination result in excluding many churches and are actually
divisions on a larger scale.

Jesus prayed to his Father that all who believe the
gospel *"may be one"* (John 17:21). The Father answered
that prayer through the work of the cross, by which we
were made one (Eph. 2:13-16). Sometimes people act as if
that prayer were prayed to them. It is an insult to our
heavenly Father and to the cross to speak now of making
the people of God one.

The apostle Paul affirmed that God's people are one:

There is one body and one Spirit—just as you were called to one hope when you were called—one Lord, one faith, one baptism; one God and Father of all, who is over all and through all and in all (Eph. 4:4-6).

This oneness is the basis of unity amongst true believers in Christ, *"the unity of the Spirit"* (Eph. 4:3). It is the unity of the Spirit and not something we produce. It is the product of submission to the one Lord. To the degree that we submit to the Word of the Lord and are "in step with the Spirit," we experience a dynamic unity of the Spirit. This unity is, first of all, with the Father, and secondarily, with the people of God. Jesus modeled this unity when he came in his Father's name (John 5:43), spoke his Father's word (John 14:24), and did only those things which he saw his Father do (John 5:19). Only this kind of unity will result in the world believing (John 17:21).

This unity is not achieved by ignoring our differences and settling for the lowest common denominator, thus treating the bulk of Scripture as though it were unimportant. A goal of scriptural unity is to *"reach unity in the faith"* (Eph. 4:13).

This unity is not limited to the invisible mystical body of Christ, but needs application amongst true believers and between true churches. (By true churches, I mean where the Scriptures are treated as God's Word, the true gospel is preached, where discipline is exercised, and the sacraments are served, thus following the basic definition that came out of the Reformation.)

The application of this unity involves recognition of other churches—acceptance of transferring members, welcoming their members at the Communion table, and acknowledging the discipline of other churches as well as welcoming their ministers. It also requires that we acknowledge churches throughout the world and accept their ministers on the same level as those in our country. They are, after all, part of God's total family of churches on earth.

When we only recognize those churches and people who dot their "i's" and cross their "t's" the way we do in the practice of our faith and interpretation of Scripture, we play God, sitting on that throne which belongs only to him (Jas. 4:11,12). The sibling rivalry that exists amongst Christians greatly hinders the gospel. It is so inconsistent for us to acknowledge great Christians who have preceded us while we reject or condemn those who subscribe to their teachings today. A few names-in-point are Augustine, Luther, Calvin, Arminius, Owen, Spurgeon, and Wesley. Followers of the teachings of each of these men include true devout followers of Jesus Christ, our brothers in Christ.

The NT teaching about the local church grants to us the freedom to practice unity between Christians and between local churches. Christendom has a crying need to address the relationship of churches to other churches from a NT point of view. The doctrine of the local church must not be practiced in a legalistic manner that fails to recognize churches that are practicing other forms of polity. Sometimes a local church can be very exclusive and amount to a denomination of one church possessing a very sectarian spirit and not the Spirit of Christ.

INTERDEPENDENT

"Independent" is often used to describe the autonomy of the local church. However, in many ways it is exactly opposite to the truth. There is an utter dependence on the Lord.

There is a dependence on the churches that have preceded us. And there is a certain interdependence on other churches. At times "independent" expresses a sectarian spirit and not the Spirit of Christ, saying we don't need our brothers.

The seventeenth-century congregationalists of New England warned against "extreme independency."[1] One's own unsanctified nature doesn't need any teaching on the local church to become an "extreme independent." Today some churches are private enterprises, men's little kingdoms built around their leaders. Some amount to a denomination of only one person.

THE SCRIPTURE ON INTER-CHURCH RELATIONSHIPS

What does the Bible say about this issue? What pattern of church relationships do we see in the NT? How did churches relate to other churches?

It was a mind-changing encounter for me when a young brother from a Gospel Hall of the Plymouth Brethren movement opened his New Testament to 1 Corinthians 1:2 which says:

> *To the church of God in Corinth, to those sanctified in Christ Jesus and called to be holy, together with all those everywhere who call on the name of the Lord....*

Both of us shared the conviction that a local assembly was a scriptural entity but I had not realized that our local assembly was "with" other local churches, including his "Gospel Hall."

In reading the NT Scriptures, we see many references to individual churches but I will note two specific ones. First, Paul addressed the *"churches in Galatia"* (Gal. 1:2). Then,

John was told to *"Write on a scroll... and send it to the seven churches..."* (Rev. 1:11). We do not find the Church of Asia or the Church of Galatia. Each of the churches in those areas was a biblical entity united to the Lord Jesus, and that union to the Lord Jesus also became the bond that united them together. None were united to Jesus through another church. Yet there was a common identification with other churches, a sense of brotherhood. They were the same kind, in the same family of churches.

They functioned together as equals. They shared the letters we now know as Scripture (Col. 4:16). They jointly chose messengers and joined in helping the poor in Jerusalem and in missionary work (2 Cor. 8). They greeted each other as equals (Rom. 16:16). They were under the authority of *the apostles*, and I don't mean those today who claim to be on the same level as the "twelve apostles" (1 Cor. 7:17). Jerusalem and Antioch met to resolve a major doctrinal problem that arose because of conflict caused by those "sent" from Antioch and those who "went" from Jerusalem (Acts 15). They practiced this mutual recognition and cooperation without organizing a hierarchy.

APPLICATION

Our common commitment must be to the same Lord. Our sense of Christian brotherhood and our common task calls for some cooperative application. However, it is this application throughout the years that has produced the organizations that, at times, became the very divisions that violated the oneness of the Christian family. These organizations became competitive rather than cooperative. They became power centers. They controlled their constituencies rather than served them. They became exclusive rather than inclusive. Often they were masters instead of servants. Religious politics has often been the order of the day. When we perceive that some have drawn a circle which excludes us, we need to draw a larger circle that includes our brethren in the family of churches.

In contrast to organized power centers we have, in the early history of the United States, an attempt to follow the NT patterns of association expressed in *The Cambridge Platform*. Those "independent" churches of New England chose elders and messengers to represent them. They conferred about Scripture, cooperation, and discipline. Their conclusions were advisory and not legislative. The alternative to "organized religion" was not "extreme independency" but free association.

Churches in free association are not over or under one another but alongside each other. They are brothers. These churches are built on Jesus Christ as their foundation. They are brought into being by the proclamation of the true gospel, not by a denomination's decree as it seeks to extend its empire or to make clones of its own kind. They are self-governing under the Lord Jesus, self-supporting and self-propagating. But they are not isolated and independent of the family of believers or the family of churches.

Each church is important! He who is "the Living One" who was dead and is alive forever, who holds the keys of death and Hades, walks in the midst of each local church (Rev. 1:18). He is in the midst with all of his life-giving and corrective power. We should not think of how churches should function in his absence but in his presence. *He* is in the midst!

In these days of megachurches, there is a tendency to think of small churches as though they were of little consequence.

Some pastors of smaller churches long for the day when they might be called to a larger church. Some megachurches have, without conscience, deliberately done all in their power to attract people from smaller churches and have used their own size and programs to compete for the "sheep." There have been instances where local churches have been devastated and missionary programs gutted by some large church's competitive programs. For pastors to properly serve God and their congregations, they must realize that their high calling is not altered by the size of the church in which they serve. Certainly, when a pastor realizes he is placed where he is by the providence of the Chief Shepherd, he will realize the significance of his ministry. It will alter how he serves the congregation and how he relates to the surrounding neighborhood. No pastor should feel his task is unimportant. A case-in-point is the ministry of A. W. Tozer, a pastor of a small congregation, the impact of which is felt around the world.

Pastors of large churches need to realize that their potential goes far beyond their congregations. John Wesley saw his potential beyond his large meetings and was a key figure in the beginning of the modern small-group movement. His meetings, and those of Whitfield, transformed Britain. Pastors of large churches are called to leadership beyond their four walls. They need to realize the power of encouragement they possess. Their visits and ministry to and in small churches can be of inestimable value. Their leadership, but not their lordship, is greatly needed.

We need each other! Can you imagine what it would be like if your church were the only church? What if the only missionary work happening was that done by your church?

Also, there are times when a church needs to invite a brother church to assist in solving problems. This was an established practice amongst the early congregationalists in England. We need to hear what *the Spirit says to the churches* (Rev. 2:29). When a church seeks such advisory help, the concept of the local church is not violated. In fact, such a practice recognizes the validity of the other churches. It is an act of humility. Much good could be accomplished by not trying to go it alone. The help a church needs may be close at hand instead of at some distant headquarters. We need to be responsible for one another and accountable to each other. Be thankful, then, for those many churches that serve alongside you.

∽ NOTES

[1] *The Cambridge Platform.* Edited by Murdy.

CHAPTER FIVE

THE CHURCH AND THE INDIVIDUAL

Where do you fit in? What are your responsibilities?

The form and function of the New Testament Church places great value on the individual. It is not a place where one loses his identity but where one finds challenge and opportunity for the fulfillment of God's purpose for an individual life.

The very word "church" means "called out." God's call comes first of all to each of us as individuals. Os Guiness said:

> Calling is the truth that God calls us to himself so decisively that everything we are, everything we do, and everything we have is invested with a special devotion, dynamism, and direction lived out as a response to his summons and service.[1]

Included in God's call to you as an individual is God's call to being a part of a local church. You will never find your potential as an individual apart from being active in a local church. The Scriptures liken the parts of the church body to hands, feet, eyes, etc. I ask you, would one be fulfilled by leaving the rest of the body or by relating to the rest of the body?

The Church is the focus of God's love (Eph. 5:25), his eternal plan. To be a part of it is to be loved and to find a life with eternal significance. His love is personal and is not measured by the size of a group.

The apostle Paul wrote, *"Now you are the body of Christ, and each one of you is a part of it"* (1 Cor. 12:27). The King James Version brings it out with more force: *"Now ye are the body of Christ, members in particular."*

Remember how one becomes that "particular" part: *"The Lord added to their number daily those who were being saved"* (Acts 2:47). *"For we were all baptized by one Spirit into one body..."* (1 Cor. 12:13). He adds and we join, but without his action our action is meaningless. Everyone he saves he places into a family of believers and in relationship with other believers.

The Church, which is his body, is indwelt by him. He lives in and through each person he forms into a church. No member of his body is insignificant or unimportant, as illustrated from the human body. Sometimes we treat believers as though they were a cup of water poured into a basin of water—the cup loses its identity. But the scriptural understanding is the very opposite, for each individual is as one's hand or foot.

This fact was forcibly brought home to me by a friend as he returned from surgery where part of his body had been removed. The surgery had taken place while he was conscious. He said it was awesome to hear the cutting and somewhat gruesome when he heard the amputated part drop into the refuse can.

Someone said, "Your hand attached to your body is extremely valuable, but amputated, it becomes garbage." Certainly that is enough for anyone to realize that each of us needs the body of believers. No one is disposable, particularly that one who seems to be a hindrance to "my" program. In fact, some of those who seem to annoy us the most are the ones we most need.

The Lord Jesus lives in and through his body, and being in his body is to be indwelt by him and to be in relationship with others. Here we find identity and worth in relationship.

Many have not applied this truth to a local congregation, only to the mystical body of Christ. Let me remind you that Paul, when writing about the body of Christ in 1 Corinthians 12, was writing to a local congregation and applied this truth to individuals in that local church.

We tend to think that only pastors, leaders, and other designated or prominent people are the important ones. If we do, we miss the point of the significance of each individual. All of us need to realize how essential each person is and cease to treat some as insignificant. *"On the contrary, those parts of the body that seem to be weaker are indispensable"* (1 Cor. 12:22).

In Jesus' description of the judgment, he said, *"...whatever you did for one of the least of these brothers of mine, you did for me"* (Matt. 25:40). In another poignant example Jesus said, *"And whoever welcomes a little child like this in my name welcomes me"* (Matt. 18:5). Consider Paul's words to Christians in dispute: *"Therefore, if you have disputes... appoint... men of little account"* (1 Cor. 6:4). Our sinful pride often prevents us from practicing our God-given relationships in this way. Almost every dispute we have can be resolved by humility. And in God's sight, the difference between the greatest and the least is too insignificant to notice. He calls us not to look down on any, nor to look up to any, but to truly be brothers and sisters to each other.

This challenges our privatism where each of us is just "doing our own thing." The authentic Christian life is realized by living in a community. No one can live a genuine Christian life in isolation from the Christian community. It is like trying to be married without a spouse.

This also eliminates the current trend of trying to be an anonymous Christian. An *anonymous Christian* is a contradiction in terms. Some belong to large churches in order to be anonymous, so no one will miss them or expect anything from them. That is simply not Christian according to scriptural teachings.

To be specific, the rich need the poor much more than the poor need the rich. Without the poor, we will remain undeveloped in our Christian life. And there are many other categories where this principle holds good. We need one another for our own spiritual growth.

Undergirding the importance of the individual is the truth Paul expressed in Galatians when he wrote, "...*the Son of God who loved me and gave himself for me*" (Gal. 2:20). The infinite God is infinite enough to love me as though there were no other person on earth, and it is legitimate to say he was thinking of me when he died on the cross. That is some of what it means to be infinite. As someone has said, "Going one on one with God is a transforming experience." You are not just a part of a group, you are the one loved and the one who needs to respond in love.

The importance of the individual is seen in Jesus' parable of the shepherd where he left ninety-nine sheep to seek for one. It is opposite to the current practices of neglecting individuals for what is seen as the common good.

The functional significance of the individual in the NT is that every single believer is a priest unto God and has access to God. And this priesthood carries with it responsibilities as well as privileges. You, as a Christian, and we, as churches, will never realize fulfillment short of the practice of the priesthood of all believers. This is what distinguishes us from other religions and cults who make the individual so subservient that individuals cannot think on their own or live according to their own consciences.

Many of the NT books were written to congregations—to laymen, if you will. They were meant to be understood by the "man on the street." Paul wrote, *"For we do not write you anything you cannot read or understand"* (2 Cor. 1:13). Jesus said that many truths were hidden from *"the wise... and revealed to little children"* (Matt. 11:25). Truth is often at the bottom of the ladder rather than at the top. While it is true that understanding comes like ascending steps, the basic understanding is available to all. It is not composed of encrypted secrets to be authoritatively interpreted by a special class. History demonstrates the power of Scripture when it is available and read by ordinary folk. The Bible belongs to you as an individual. When the understanding of Scriptures is left to revelations by "prophets" or mystic voices "in the spirit," we become enslaved to some form of cultic gnosticism, we cease to think for ourselves, we forfeit our freedom of conscience, and we deny both the character of Scripture and the illuminating ministry of the Holy Spirit. No one has the right to control our thinking or compel us to violate our own consciences.

Some exploit people instead of equipping them for service. The Church is intended to mobilize us into ministry to God, to other believers, and to the world of lost people.

Learn to be yourself, part of the family of God, a member of the body of Christ, a priest unto God. Face your own identity crisis. Look into the mirror of God's Word and discover yourself as loved, a child of God, one of God's priests. Know what your gift is, then use your God-given gift in the family of God. Listen to God's call to you. Sometimes his call transcends "gifting," such as in the case of Moses, who was called to do what he was not gifted to do (Exod. 4:10, 11).

Respond to your Lord. *You* are the one he loves. *You* are the one he calls. *Only you* can answer him, and *only you* can be that body part in your church where he has called you to be.

ᴖ NOTES

[1] Guinness. *The Call*.

CHAPTER SIX

CHURCH MEMBERSHIP

I don't want to join anything! I want to keep my freedom. Who instituted church membership?

A normal New Testament Church requires a group of committed people in order to function as a healthy body. A healthy body needs each of its members.

Is it possible to have a body that has no members? Theoretically, I suppose one can theorize about a body that has no hands, no feet, no ears, etc., but at best that is a very abnormal situation. To apply this biblical analogy of a church to a physical body, what is a hand or foot when not attached to a body?

It is a wonderful thing to be a part of a family of believers, to have an identity bigger than one's self. Within that family, it is a wonderful thing to care for and be cared for by others, and to be a member of a group of people who are mutually accountable to each other. It is membership in such a local church that provides the environment necessary to one's normal development as a follower of Christ.

THE ORIGIN OF THE TERM "MEMBER" OR "MEMBERSHIP"

The word "member" is derived from the apostle Paul's usage of a body's members to describe the Church. This figure of speech suits a local church, since a body with its members makes a person visible. People were joined to a particular body of believers to experience and practice "body life." Church membership is a fact of life without which a church does not exist though that membership may be informal. That is, every church requires a group of committed people to even be a church.

This is self-evident, for the mere casual association of Christians will not produce or maintain a church any more than a load of building material dumped on a lot can constitute a building.

Formal membership is where people commit themselves to a church body in writing or public commitment. Informal membership is having a heart commitment to a church body without expressing it in any official way.

Commitment is the essence of what is meant by membership. It is a commitment to the Lord Jesus to serve God in union with others. It is also a joint commitment to a family of believers with whom we live out our commitment to our Lord. Our commitment is to the message and the vision of one's congregation. It is also a commitment to the missionaries who have been sent out from the congregation. If it is just a commitment to the leader, the church will greatly suffer when there is a change of leadership. When the commitment is just to the leader, there is a tendency to develop a cult-like loyalty to that leader. In many churches there is a frequent change of pastors, and if our commitment is to the pastor, both the church and the pastors will suffer. Some denominations have a rule that no pastor shall stay longer than five years in order to make certain that the commitment is to the Lord and to the congregation.

To try to recover the form and function of the NT Church without being vitally united to the Lord Jesus and a body of believers is to play word games.

THE CAMBRIDGE PLATFORM

In *The Cambridge Platform*, written in 1649, the elders and messengers of the churches assembled in Cambridge, Massachusetts and wrote of the significance of church membership. People joined their local churches by entering into a covenant with each other, committing themselves to serve God and one another. One of the purposes of their mutual covenant was to make certain a congregation was composed of truly regenerate people. It was to prevent nominal church membership which has afflicted churches throughout Church history. Their mutual covenant spelled out what it meant to be an active part of one of their churches. Church membership was not a meaningless name on a church register. It formed the basis for meaningful church discipline. Without church membership, church discipline is rendered almost inoperable.

A FASCINATING EXAMPLE

A fascinating example of a membership covenant was made by the Pilgrims in Salem, Mass., in 1636. It read:

1 First wee avowe the Lord to be our God, and ourselves his people in the truth and simplicitie of our spirits.

2 We give our selves to the Lord Jesus Christ, and the word of his grace, for the teaching ruleing and sancti-

fyeing of us in the matters of worship, and Conversation, resolveing to cleave to him alone for life and glorie; and oppose all contrarie wayes, canons and constitutions of men in his worship.

3 Wee promise to walke with our brethren and sisters in this Congregation with all watchfullness and tenderness, avoyding all jelousies, suspsitions, backbyteings, censurings, provoakings, secrete risings of spirite against them; but in all offences to follow the rule of the Lord Jesus, and to beare and forbeare, give and forgive as he hath taught us.

4 In publick or in private, we will willing doe nothing to the ofence of the Church but will be willing to take advise for our selves and ours as ocasion shalbe presented.

5 Wee will not in the Congregation be forward eyther to shew oure owne gifts or parts in speaking or scrupling, or there discover the fayling of our brethren or sisters butt attend an oderly cale there unto; knowing how much the Lord may be dishonoured and his Gospell in the profession of it, sleighted, by our distempers, and weaknesses in publyck.

6 Wee bynd ourselves to studdy the advancement of the Gospell in all truth and peace, both in regard of those that are within, or without, noe way sleighting our sister Churches, but useing theire Counsell as need shalbe: nor laying a stumbling block before any, noe not the Indians, whose good we desire to promote and soe to converse, as we may avoyd the verrye appearance of evill.

7 We hearbye promise to carrye our selves in all lawfull obedience, to those that are over us, in Church or

common weale, knowing how well pleasing it will be to the Lord, that they should have incouragement in theire places, by our not greiveing theyre spirites through our Irregularities.

8 Wee resolve to approve our selves to the Lord in our perticular calings, shunning ydleness as the bane of any state, nor will wee deale hardly, or oppressingly with any, wherein we are the Lord's stewards:

9 alsoe promyseing to our best abilitie to teach our children and servants, the knowledge of God and his will, that they may serve him also; and all this, not by any strength of our owne, but by the Lord Christ, whose bloud we desire may sprinkle this our Covenant made in his name.[1]

AN ANALOGY

One day while listening to the radio, I heard the speaker quote an effective analogy by Kent Hughes of Wheaton, Illinois, who said:

> The church today is filled with ecclesiastical hitchhikers. The hitchhiker's thumb says you buy the car, pay for the repairs, upkeep and fill the car with gas, and I'll ride with you. If you have an accident, you are on your own and I'll probably sue.

So it is today with the credo of so many church attendees. They say, "You go to the meetings, serve on the boards and committees; you grapple with the issues and do the work of the church and pay the bills. I'll come along for the ride but if things do not suit me, I'll criticize and complain and will probably bail out. My thumb is always out for a better ride."

There are hitchhikers who attend one church for the preaching, send their children to another church for the dynamic youth program, and go to a third church for a "small group." Church hitchhikers have a telling vocabulary. "I go to church," or "I attend but never belong to," or "I'm never a member." So today, at the turn of the millennium, we have a phenomenon unthinkable in any other century: "Churchless Christians."

Somebody has said there are "two kinds of people in the church, the pillars and the caterpillars. The pillars hold things up and the caterpillars crawl in and out every week." The point is a pungent rebuke to uncommitted Christians.

MEMBERSHIP IS IMPLICIT IN JESUS' MANDATE OF THE LOCAL CHURCH.

In Jesus' first mention of the function of a local church, he, speaking of the church's self-discipline, said,

> *But if he will not listen, take one or two others along, so that 'every matter may be established by the testimony of two or three witnesses.' If he refuses to listen to them, tell it to the church; and if he refuses to listen even to the church... treat him as you would a pagan..."* (Matt. 18:16,17).

From this we can clearly deduce that:

1. *people in a congregation are responsible to and for one another;*

2. *inner relationships are of great importance;*

3. *such a group is responsible to a clearly defined body of people, i.e. people are either "in" or "out" of a definable group (brother or pagan);*

4. *the church is local, since it would be an impossible job to tell the whole world;*

5. *there is no higher court of appeal to any ecclesiastical hierarchy.*

LEADERS GIVE AN ACCOUNT TO GOD.

"Remember your leaders..." (Heb. 13:7).

Obey your leaders and submit to their authority. They keep watch over you as men who must give an account. Obey them so that their work will be a joy, not a burden, for that would be of no advantage to you (13:17).

These are *your* leaders. If one cannot identify one's leaders, one will simply go from leader to leader until a leader tells him what he wants to hear. When John the Baptist was reminded that his congregation was leaving him to follow Jesus, he said, *"A man can receive only what is given him from heaven"* (John 3:27). It is my conviction that the Chief Shepherd entrusts specific sheep to certain leaders and gives leaders to specific sheep for whom they will give an account on judgment day. We who are in leadership need to ponder that thought.

A CONGREGATION IS EXHORTED TO KNOW ITS LEADERS.

"Now we ask you, brothers, to respect [know] *those who work hard among you..."* (1 Thess. 5:12). These whom the congregation is to "know" are identified as those who labor "among you" (locally and not everywhere), who are over you, and who admonish you.

WE ARE RESPONSIBLE TO AND FOR ONE ANOTHER

We can't be responsible for everybody in the world or even in a particular locale but only in the congregation of which we are a part. God held the Corinthian congregation responsible for an immoral member (1 Cor. 5). Certain widows were the specific responsibility of a local congregation (1 Tim. 5). (This wasn't a worldwide widow ministry.) In the Spirit's letters to the seven churches, those local congregations were responsible for their members: *"Yet you have a few people..."* (Rev. 3:4). Paul speaks of how members care for one another:

> *Epaphras, who is one of you and a servant of Christ Jesus.... is always wrestling in prayer for you, that you may stand firm in all the will of God, mature and fully assured* (Col. 4:12).

That is the practice of church membership.

One part of responsible caring for one another is discipline, so I ask you this: Have you ever tried to exercise church discipline where there is no membership? The person being disciplined just says, "I don't belong here anyway. You are not my pastor." Such individuals simply go uncorrected and attend elsewhere. The disciplinary process is frustrated and another body becomes infected by the undisciplined person.

WE ARE TOLD TO RECEIVE ONE ANOTHER

"Accept one another..." (Rom. 15:7). To be so accepted one must be a part of those described as "one another." The situation in Rome involved receiving people of different

races and social classes, so we find slaves and slave owners were exhorted to *"greet one another with a holy kiss"* (Rom. 16:16). It included an *"equal concern"* for everyone and not just our own particular clique (1 Cor. 12:25). Letters are written to congregations and leaders of congregations about receiving specific people (Rom. 16:2; Phil. 2:29; Col. 3:13; Philem. 2; John 8:1-11). One house-church is specifically told not to receive those denying the deity of Jesus Christ (2 John 10). Entrance into the receiving group was not all that easy for Saul/Paul (Acts 9:26). In times of persecution receiving just anybody could cost the lives or imprisonment of the rest of the congregation.

GOD ADDED TO, AND PEOPLE JOINED
THE NUMBER

"And the Lord added to their number daily those who were being saved" (Acts 2:47). It was an act of the Lord, and it was a specific number to which they were added, not a nebulous group. *"No one else dared join them..."* [the word for "join" meaning "to glue," "cement," or "join"— Vine[2]] (Acts 5:13). It certainly meant more than a casual association which, in our time, is often mislabeled "church membership," a kind of thing in which I wish no one believed. Joining is the responsive action of believers. People were counted and others counted on them. (Did you ever notice how many specific numbers of people are identified in the book of Acts? Some observed that the primary counting took place at the prayer meeting!)

Paul, writing to the divided Corinthian congregation (the division of which is difficult to understand unless it was intended to be a coherent whole), said:

I appeal to you, brothers, in the name of our Lord Jesus Christ, that all of you agree with one another so that there may be no divisions among you and that you may be perfectly united" ["joined together" KJV; Gk.: "to adjust thoroughly; to knit together, unite completely" *The Analytical Greek Lexicon*] (1 Cor. 1:10).

Paul wrote about "the whole church" coming together (1 Cor. 14:23). This is quite different from the scattered sheep of today.

Membership, whether formal or informal, demonstrates that a congregation is a definable body of people. People are either "in" or "out." No one can be "put out" of something one is not "in." The Corinthian congregation, as a body, was rebuked for tolerating the immoral man in 1 Corinthians 5. Leaders must know those for whom they are responsible, and followers must know to whom they are responsible.

MEMBERS HAD A VITAL INTERACTION WITH ONE ANOTHER.

Being joined together was a living reality (1 Cor. 12). Jesus, the head of the body, ministered to its various members through its members. No one could experience a normal Christian life apart from being a part of the corporate life of a congregation.

Each of us is called to pray and prepare for ministry to one another. One cannot say of another, "I don't need you" (1 Cor. 12:21). Ministry, by divine design, flows from one member to another: *"Let the word of Christ dwell in you richly as you teach and admonish one another with all wisdom..."* (Col. 3:16). This is not the picture of pulpit-to-pew ministry but that of one member to another.

Chapter 12 of 1 Corinthians describes a vibrant vital interaction of members within a local church. In this passage the functioning of the gifts of the Spirit is normal to a church's life. Apart from a local church, these become a law unto themselves. Prophecies are not judged by others. That which is accomplished is not conserved, and there is little, if any, net gain.

MEMBERSHIP WAS MODELED IN THE NEW TESTAMENT.

Paul wrote to the Colossians, *"...Onesimus, our faithful and dear brother, who is one of you* [a member of the church at Colosse]*... Epaphras, who is one of you* [a member of the church at Colosse]*..."* (Col. 4:9,12), even though these men were in Rome.

JESUS IS THE IDEAL PASTOR/SHEPHERD.

Jesus knew his sheep and they knew his voice. Pastors today need to know for whom they are responsible and believers should know to whom they are accountable. When James tells the sick to call for the elders to come and pray for them (James 5:14), the passage clearly indicates there is a committed relationship between the elders and the congregation. The context of this passage suggests that the elders' ministry included both the spiritual as well as the physical. It is interesting that they weren't exhorted to seek someone with the "gift of healing."

A GRAPHIC EXAMPLE

Seven of us were climbing Mount Hood. One person had never climbed before. Our climbing rope tied us all together. We were in a very steep icy part of the final ascent of a place called "the chute." Our new climber was frightened and wanted to "hug the mountain" rather than staying perpendicular, thus using his weight to make his spiked crampons grip the slippery slope. No amount of talking could persuade him from leaning into the mountain. However, within moments his feet went out from under him and he started to slide. The rest of us dug in with our ice axes, and our rope held him.

The significance of being roped together was evident to all. That is my point about being a committed part of a church. We are roped together by our commitment to Christ and to one another. The Lord only knows the dreadful casualty rate of those who just go it alone.

"ONE ANOTHER""

These very words are used about fifty times in the NT to describe the interactive lives of members of a congregation. They are translated from a Greek "reciprocal pronoun"[3] that describes the interactions of an identifiable group. Sometimes the Greek word is translated "each other" as in 1 Thess. 5:13: *"...Live in peace with each other."* The identifiable group is designated *"the church of the Thessalonians"* in 1:1, and called *"brothers"* (5:12). Another example reads:

> *We ought always to thank God for you, brothers, and rightly so, because your faith is growing more and more, and the love every one of you has for each other is increasing* (2 Thess. 1:3).

The repeated use of the Greek word indicates an identifiable group to which one belongs and does not include just anybody or everybody.

OBSERVATIONS

Romans 16 is relevant: There were a *number* of churches in Rome, not just one in that city. These churches met in different houses (vs. 5), and the churches that met in these houses were described as *"all the saints with them"* (14, 15). Then the original text reads *"the ones of Aristobulus"* and *"the ones of Narcissus"* (10,11), which the NIV interpretatively translates as of *"the household of"* but probably describes other house churches. It is evident that different believers in Rome were a part of this or that house church and were included in the greeting to those particular house churches. It is significant that these were separate house churches and were not simply described as one church.

THE ALTERNATIVE

The alternative to being a committed part of an identifiable group is to function as an individual or to try to relate as one having a kind of universal membership in the invisible mystical body of Christ. However, the only viable option that will enable the individual to mature in Christ is to be a committed part of a congregation. Every one of us needs to be accountable to and responsible for our fellow Christians. This includes all ministers and missionaries, some of whom are the worst offenders as they function in an unaccountable freelance manner.

May every one of us as believers commit ourselves to serving God in the corporate life of a congregation and actively join together in the great work of making Christ known. Accepting one's spiritual family and being responsible for one's brothers and sisters is essential for normal spiritual development. As God's plan is that the human race be placed within families, so it is that the redeemed race should be a part of spiritual families called churches.

NOTES

[1] Walker. *Creeds and Platforms of Congregationalism.* 116.

[2] Vine. *Vine's Complete Expository Dictionary.* 334

[3] Robertson. *Grammar of Greek New Testament.* 692.

CHAPTER SEVEN

CHURCH DISCIPLINE

What is a garden uncultivated? What is a tree unpruned? What are clothes unwashed? What is a child left to himself? How can a student realize fulfillment without the "disciplines" of school? And what is a church without discipline?

For a church to function according to the pattern in the New Testament, it must accept the responsibility of self-discipline. Discipline isn't only correction, it is training.

> But who is it that wishes the Church to tolerate a little sin here and there? It is the devil. And he does not love the Church; he hates it. Why does he wish sin to be tolerated? Because he knows that it means the ruination of the Church and the destruction of souls.[1]

Why do I include this chapter on church discipline? The power to discipline defines various forms of church government. For a church to be a church, it must have the power to discipline its members. On the subject of discipline, Lenski says that if that congregation had failed in the matter of discipline, "Corinth would have been lost to the church."[2] This is essentially what is being said to the church in Ephesus in Revelations 2:5 which warns that they need to either repent or have their lampstand removed. Discipline is essential to the integrity of the Church, to its very holy character as the people of God. It is inherent in Jesus' charter of the local church in Matthew 18. Without the power of discipline, a church doesn't have power to exist. The power to discipline defines the local church and, by that same token, this power distinguishes the local church from all those groups for whom discipline comes from the hierarchy. It is absolutely essential for recognition and cooperation with other churches. (Some churches cooperate on the basis of a common designation, such as Presbyterian, Baptist, etc., but in the NT, discipline is essential to recognition and cooperation.) It is a part of moving from the "invisible" church to the "visible" church.

One of the marks of a true church, according to some of the leaders of the Reformation, is the practice of church discipline. Church discipline is God's discipline carried out through God's people. It is impossible to develop into a true disciple of Jesus Christ without discipline. The connection between discipleship and discipline is self-evident. Church discipline is a practice of being the "body of Christ," of one hand washing the other. We need each other. We are our brother's keepers. We are responsible to and for one another.

"Discipline" or "chasten" is translated from *paideia* which means to "child train." God's love, not his wrath, is the motive behind discipline (Heb. 12:6). Discipline is not punishment. Punishment has to do with the past, with what happened. Discipline, or chastening, has to do with the present and the future. Discipline is love manifested, and its purpose is restoration and maturity. *"He who spares the rod hates his son, but he who loves him is careful to discipline him"* (Prov. 13:24).

Those who do not truly love the person needing to be

disciplined are disqualified from administering discipline. And in direct correlation, people who do not recognize that love is the motive behind discipline will not receive discipline. If we do not realize that God's love is behind such discipline we will become defensive, even bitter. It is absolutely essential to realize that God's love is behind his discipline because all the difficulties of life we need to receive have a "child-training" purpose for us. Those who react otherwise are described as being like Esau (Heb. 12:14-17).

It is an unfortunate believer who attends a church where discipline is not practiced. *"Whoever loves discipline loves knowledge, but he who hates correction is stupid"* (Prov. 12:1). *"A wise son heeds his father's instruction, but a mocker does not listen to a rebuke"* (Prov. 13:1).

Paul's instruction to Timothy, who was thought to be the pastor in Ephesus at the time, was:

> *Preach the Word; be prepared in season and out of season; correct, rebuke and encourage—with great patience and careful instruction. For the time will come* [has come] *when men will not put up with sound doctrine* (2 Tim. 4:2,3).

Instead of leaving a church when we are rebuked, we need to appreciate those who love us enough to tell us the cleansing truth.

When speaking of practicing NT discipline, one key word is "patience." All of us need to remember God's severe discipline of Moses when he lost patience with his people. Patience is sometimes seen as weakness, but nothing seems to take more strength than patience.

While God's discipline of us as his children far exceeds

the functions of a church, a number of things are specifically the responsibility of the local church.

The Lord Jesus' instruction on the form and function of the church deals with discipline in Matthew 18:15-20. It is important to note the context. It is preceded by a section on seeking a lost sheep and followed by our Lord's longest and strongest teaching on forgiveness. We are the society of the forgiven. It is a part of the primary mandate for the local church, where the Lord is in the very midst of the people gathered in his name. One of its purposes is to maintain harmony amongst the "brothers." The ultimate action is by the "agree[ment]" of the gathering and, of course, this must include an agreement with the Lord who is in their midst. But it also includes a united group of people accepting the responsibility for the correction of its members. Excusing sin must not be confused with forgiveness.

At no time should discipline express the desire of a congregation to exercise power to control others such as the cults do. Discipline's motive is love, not power. It must assume an attitude of forgiveness on the part of those exercising discipline.

> The individual is alone responsible for his sin so long as no one else knows about it, but as soon as it is revealed to the church that body becomes responsible for it.[3]

We see the application of discipline in some of Paul's letters. Some are named as those already disciplined in the letters to Timothy. Some whose sins are identified and are not publicly disciplined are also identified. Some are disciplined by God's Word and not any direct action of the church, examples of which we see in 1 Corinthians 6:1; 11:31, 32; and Ephesians 4:25,28,31.

Discipline is by the Word of God. Here are two scriptural affirmations: 1) Jesus said, *"You are already clean because of the word I have spoken to you"* (John 15:3); and 2) Jesus uses the water of his Word to cleanse his Church (Eph. 5:26). All of us need to trust in the cleansing power of his Word as well as to submit to it.

The instructive example of church discipline in the NT is the man living immorally with his stepmother (1 Cor. 5:1-5). It is apparent that Paul spoke of himself as being "present" in this matter of discipline, which probably refers to his presence by means of the letter he sent to them.

One reason for such discipline was the contagiousness of sin: *"Don't you know that a little yeast works through the whole batch of dough?"* (5:6) Therefore, discipline is not applied because we are better than the person being disciplined, but because we are vulnerable to the same "disease."

Paul was grieved about the sinful person and the way the Corinthians not only tolerated this situation but actually boasted about it. Paul loved the congregation *and* the man. Lenski says Paul's letter was "dripping with tears." Lenski, in his commentary on 1 and 2 Corinthians,[4] profitably comments extensively on this matter. (Included will be repeated references to his comments.)

The issues involved include the dreadful effect of the sin on the life of the immoral person, the pollution of the congregation, the obedience of the congregation to the Lord, the loss of true spiritual joy, the example it sets for others, and the destruction of what it means to be a congregation celebrating the NT Passover. If we grasp these things and they grasp us, we will experience a holy horror of such sinfulness, enough horror that we must act in love and obedience to bring about discipline.

In Lenski's perception, Paul's letter came as a motion to a legally convened assembly (as supported by technical Greek words), a motion on which the church members needed to act. They were to do this by the authority of the Lord Jesus as well as in union with him. They ultimately acted on this motion with a congregational vote, indicated by the Greek word for the "majority" (2 Cor. 2:6). Under the old covenant, the accusing person had to throw the first stone, but here each member of the congregation is called upon to cast a vote of discipline. The Word shows that it was not unanimous, which also tells us that they didn't function by unanimous consent, as some idealize.

Lenski said:

> All hierarchical notions are far from Paul's thinking and acting. Throughout the case the primary position belonged to the congregation. It had to pass the resolution that expelled the man.[5]

This conforms to the pattern set forth by our Lord in Matthew 18. "This shows that each congregation is autonomous, but it is under Christ when it is exercising its autonomy."[6]

Moreover, the apostle Paul makes his forgiveness of the sinful party contingent on the action of that local church, *"If you forgive anyone, I also forgive him"* (2 Cor. 2:10). Certainly, this is opposite to a religious hierarchy.

Paul's patience in this matter stands out as an example for all of us. He loved, he prayed, he sent a letter, and he sent a messenger. There was no "knee-jerk" response but a prayerful, careful, patient entreaty.

Often, we go from one extreme to another, from tolerance of sin to a legalistic hardness that makes no place for restoration. So Paul had to write to them, and I believe to us, to fully receive repentant people. Lenski points up a biblical pattern: First, mention the sin and not the sinner; second, if he does not repent, mention the sin and the sinner by name; but if he repents, we should not mention either the sin or the sinner's name relative to the sin and the disciplinary action.

Another relevant passage is in Galatians 6. When Paul wrote to the Galatians about correcting and restoring people who have fallen into sin, he required that the restoring person be both humble and spiritual. The person must be spiritual, manifesting the fruit of the Spirit about which Paul had just written, and the restoring person must be humble enough to know that he himself could fall into the same thing. He uses the word "restore," which has various meanings. I think the most applicable one here is that suggested by Kenneth Wuest, who sees it as the act of adjusting a bone that is out of place. I am afraid some of our attempts to restore the fallen are more like the efforts of a "horse doctor" or a "quack."

The book of Galatians is deeply involved in the difference between the old covenant and the new. Under the old covenant, such an offending person may have been stoned to death. How different things are under the new covenant. However, neither covenant is tolerant of sin. Sin must be dealt with. Discipline is absolutely essential. It must start with our own self-discipline (2 Tim. 2:19). Under the new covenant, it must reflect the grace and forgiveness of God as we endeavor to "wash another's feet." It is the responsibility of all believers as we function as our brothers' keepers. It must not be left to the pastor, as though his job description included being the official policeman.

May we all stand in the fear of God and be awed by what it means to be disciplined by a church—to be turned out from under the canopy of grace that overspreads God's Church and be handed over to Satan. This can be a matter of life or death. Understanding this, one cannot help but feel that it is a wonderful thing to be a part of one of Christ's churches.

May we be convicted of our sins and not merely condemned by them. May we be moved in loving grief over the sins of the members in our congregations. May we not suppose that thundering sermons against sin constitute biblical discipline. May we lovingly care enough to confront those who both confess Christ as Savior yet continue in sin.

May God give us a vision of his holiness and a passion like that of Jesus, of whom it was said, *"Zeal for your house will consume me"* (John 2:17). In zeal he took a whip and cleansed his Father's house of the money changers. May we also be possessed by love-tempered zeal for the holiness of his house.

How grateful we should be for those caring enough for us to guide, correct, and confront. I can remember a conversation with David Augsberger in which he said that he wished he had never written *Freedom through Forgiveness* because he said it failed to embody the truth in another of his books, *Caring Enough to Confront*. Personally, I am deeply indebted to a lady who cared enough to confront me as a teenager about my waywardness. She personally contacted me through a letter about my conduct that was known to no one else. She promised not to tell anyone if I would respond to the correction of her letter. I heard the voice of my Savior in her letter and she told no one, for which I am in her debt. I often wonder how different my life would have been without her "cleansing" words.

∾ NOTES

[1] Pethrus. *Christian Church Discipline*. 25.

[2] Lenski. *The Interpretation of I and II Corinthians*. 877.

[3] Pethrus. Op. cit. 28.

[4] Lenski. Op. cit. 205-226; 862-890.

[5] Op. cit. 879.

[6] Op. cit. 887.

CHAPTER EIGHT

WHO NEEDS TO ATTEND CHURCH?

One of the essential definitions of local church autonomy is a "gathered church." That is inherent to the word "church." It is an assembly. It has to be this to function.

When one realizes Who has promised to gather with those who come together in his name, one has every reason to attend. He is more important than anything we might conjure up to excuse our absence.

When one realizes that our Lord's plan is to minister to us through the different members of the family, it is obvious we cannot consider giving up "meeting together" (Heb. 10:25).

Evidently, Satan realizes these things and for that reason does all he can to keep us away from the gathering of our spiritual family. (How many notable Christians do you know who don't make regular church attendance a habit of life?)

I sat across from the lawyer as he took the deposition. The state of Oregon contested the need and right of prisoners to gather for a regular church service. In preparation for this day with the prisoners' attorney, I had gathered materials gleaned from prisoners in Vietnam. The prisoners in Vietnam shared what a gathering of believers meant to them: The fellowship sustained them and enabled them to resist brainwashing, etc. Some spoke of gathering for Communion with prisoners in adjacent cells by thumping messages to their fellow prisoners as they jointly participated in the Communion which was necessarily conceptual. The prisoners' attorney was building a case to show that forbidding prisoners from gathering together for a Christian service was a cruel and unusual punishment. Those prisoners from Vietnam both inspired others and challenged all who read their words to come to a deeper appreciation of what it means to attend a worship service.

An empty building filled with empty pews named after the people who have gathered in the past does not constitute a church. Writing about churches without writing about attendance and participation gives a false message. God's called-together people constitute a church.

As already noted, Congregationalism has defined itself since the sixteenth century as "the gathered church." Unless we define a church as a "gathered church," we end up emphasizing buildings instead of people. Whether we are talking about the gatherings of old in the catacombs beneath Rome, the "underground" house meetings in places such as China today, or church gatherings as we know them in America, gathering together as members of the Christian community is the issue.

OUR NEED FOR ONE ANOTHER

"I am a Christian, but I don't go to church. You don't have to go to church to be a Christian," was the woman's reply as I endeavored to do some door-to-door evangelism.

My reply came right out of a recent experience with a broken wrist. "That's true," I said, "but you can never live a normal Christian life apart from gathering with your brothers and sisters. I have recently struggled with a broken wrist. I had to learn to tie my shoes with my left hand. I learned that each member of my body needs another part of my body to function normally, and it is the same way in the body of Christ."

CHURCHES DON'T SAVE PEOPLE, BUT SAVED PEOPLE GO TO CHURCH

People often ask questions like, "Do you have to go to church to be a Christian? Doesn't the Bible teach that God is everywhere? Can't I read my Bible at home?" Questions like these are usually asked by people who are not seeking answers but excuses for not attending church.

Others reason, "I don't get much out of church attendance. I already know what is going to be said. I feel closer to God when I am out in nature. People at church aren't very friendly. I don't like crowds. I feel more guilty when I go to church. I don't like being pressured by people at church. There are a lot of hypocrites in churches." These and other excuses are as hypocritical as those being used for excuses not to attend.

MORE THAN A PILE OF BUILDING MATERIAL

Some reason this way because they have never moved beyond being merely a part of an audience to being a part of a church. Charles Jefferson, in a lecture at Yale, said:

> A sharp distinction ought to be made between a church and an audience…. An audience is a crowd; a church is a family of believers. An audience is a heap of stones; a church is a temple….

These words complement the Scripture that says we are *"being built together to become a dwelling in which God lives by his Spirit"* (Eph. 2:22).

And, of course, being so fit together requires commitment and continual close association.

WHERE WE ARE BEING SAVED

The "saved" are also in the process of being saved. As C. S. Lewis noted:

> He works on us in all sorts of ways. But above all, He works on us through each other. Men are mirrors, or 'carriers' of Christ to other men. Usually it is those who know Him that bring Him to others. That is why the Church, the whole body of Christians showing Him to one another, is so important. It is so easy to think that Church has a lot of different objects—education, building, missions, holding services.... The Church exists for no other purpose but to draw men into Christ, to make them little Christs. If they are not doing that, all the cathedrals, clergy, missions, sermons, even the Bible itself, are simply a waste of time. God became man for no other purpose. It is even doubtful, you know, whether the whole universe was created for any other reason.[1]

Church is the dynamic interaction of sinners in the process of salvation. It is a spiritual support group with a love commitment to each one. It is like a group of mountain climbers roped together as they ascend the slippery slopes. It is the fusion of different lives, making them more than the sum of their individual lives. In the OT, God placed his name in a designated place (Deut. 12). In the NT, he has placed his name in the gathering of believers, and he personally promised his presence to such a gathering (Matt. 18:20). All social, economic, and racial differences are erased by the significance of his person. The ground is level at the foot of the cross where we gather in the name of Jesus, meaning that there is a complete equality within the congregation.

Salvation in the NT is expressed in three tenses: we have been saved, we are being saved, and we shall be saved. The Church is an instrument God uses in the process of our being saved. Yes, the local church has saving power as it acts in union with its head.

I remember the Swedish tenor, Einar Waermo, telling about a visit to a factory in which they manufactured those little, old-fashioned, wooden clothespins. Waermo said he had always wondered how they made them so smooth. At the factory he found out. The wooden clothespins were tumbled together in what looked like a large washing machine. There they lost all their rough edges as they tumbled together. Waermo said, "Now I see what church is all about."

NECESSARY FOR A NORMAL CHRISTIAN LIFE

As one cannot have family life without a family, or have a married life without a spouse, so no one can experience a normal Christian life in isolation. Everyone needs a church family, and the Church needs every Christian. An essential part of the Christian life is one's participation in a church. As Thomas Merton said, "No man is an island".[2] Isolation has been shown to have serious psychological consequences in development, emotional health, and even in the perception of reality. The same can be said for believers who seek to live a Christian life in isolation from a spiritual family.

Look at the dynamics: In the law it says, *"Five of you will chase a hundred, and a hundred of you will chase ten thousand…"* (Lev. 26:8), and Solomon wrote, *"…A cord of three strands is not quickly broken"* (Eccl. 4:12). The reason many do not experience this strength is because they have mistaken casual association for the genuine article of acceptance, commitment, and accountability experienced by those who move from being spectators to being a part of the team.

It is Jesus' plan for us to *"come together"* (Matt. 18:20). He said the seal of authenticity and testimony to the world is how we *"love one another"* (John 13:35). That seal is stamped on the "birth certificate" of everyone genuinely born into God's family (1 John 3:14). We are family.

Every person being saved was added to a congregation (Acts 2:47). The gathering was described with the Greek word *koinonia*, a word meaning a new dimension in relationships. In essence, it describes people in joint participation. Some scholars suggest that it is "buying into something." It certainly doesn't describe a passive observation of religious activities. The Protestant Reformation moved church life from observation to participation.

Almost all churches of various convictions agree on the necessity of the sacrament of the Lord's Table, without which, according to the Reformers, the Church does not exist. It is commonly labeled "Communion," which may well be translated, "joint participation." None of the usual substitutes, such as radio and television, provide such participation which was instituted by our Lord (1 Cor. 11:23-26).

SIGN OF TRUE DISCIPLESHIP

The pattern of the early Christians challenges each of us; theirs is a pattern of close relationships. It is a relationship so meaningful that we *"lay down our lives"* for our brothers (1 John 3:16). (Some of us can't even lay down an hour or two to gather with our family.) Our love has to be reflected by a desire to gather together with our spiritual families to worship the Lord who so loved us that he came into this world to die for us.

Years ago I was in the hospital for almost a year. There I experienced the loss of regularly meeting with my brothers and sisters. Since then I find it almost unbelievable that some who profess to be Christians place little or no value on the gathering of believers.

Some have said, "Let the church be the church." For that to happen, we, as members of the Lord's body, must be active members of the Church. For the "body" to make the invisible presence of the Lord visible, it is essential that each of us function in our relationship to both our head and our fellow-members.

Practical realities demonstrate our need to be an active part of a congregation. It is difficult to keep track of people and their needs when they don't regularly gather together. It is impossible to fulfill the Scriptures describing the responsibilities between leaders and followers (Heb. 13:17) if we are not a part of a regular gathering for worship of our Lord.

OUR MUTUAL RESPONSIBILITY

Also, as believers in Christ, we are responsible for each other. The issue is not only what we get out of the gathering but what we contribute to the gathering. We gather with concern for the spiritual and physical well-being of each member of our spiritual family, something that is not expressed if we are spiritual "lone rangers." We are "our brothers' keepers."

Paul writes about the *"whole church"* (1 Cor. 14:23) and asks, *"What then shall we say, brothers? When you*

101

come together, everyone has a hymn, or a word of instruction..." (1 Cor. 14:26). Can a church be "whole" when part of the congregation is absent? (There is no possible meaning here but that of a local church.) Paul visualizes a time of mutual instruction and encouragement, a time of edification. As Christ-followers, we cannot participate in this experience if we are not there. Without such participation, we not only do not exercise our particular ministry, but we ourselves will not develop as God intended. Bearing our responsibility is essential to our own growth. Our very presence is an encouragement to others—and our absence a discouragement.

Paul wrote to Timothy:

> *Although I hope to come to you soon, I am writing you these instructions so that, if I am delayed, you will know how people ought to conduct themselves in God's household, which is the church of the living God, the pillar and foundation of the truth* (1 Tim. 3:14,15).

Paul had an awesome concept of God's Church. Do we? Being a part of Christ's Church is being built on the foundation and being a part of the pillar (the visible testimony of Christ's incarnation and redemption). It is pointless to speak of how we conduct ourselves *in* God's household if we don't even bother to conduct ourselves *to the gathering* of God's household.

MAKING THE INVISIBLE VISIBLE

As J. I. Packer says:

> The Church becomes visible in its local assemblies, each of which is the body of Christ in manifestation.... It becomes visible by its association, fellowship, disci-

pline, and witness, by the preaching and sharing of God's Word which it sponsors, by its administration of the sacraments of entry and continuance according to Christ's command, and by its commitment to the work which the Master gave it to do.[3]

Being a "pillar of truth" is being a part of the testimony to the gospel. The pillar is a visible witness. This requires that we subordinate our personal interests in order to gather with our spiritual family. What kind of testimony do we have if it is not important enough for us to gather with God's people for the hearing of God's Word? How often have we ever seen someone who didn't attend church effectively witness to others about Christ? Have we ever considered the effect on our own families and relatives if we don't bother to meet with our spiritual family? How many people do we know who aren't regularly participating in the church gathering and yet consistently reading the Scripture and praying with their families at home? If they take seriously what they are reading at home, they will gather regularly with other believers. And if they are not assembling together as believers, their children will probably not even be reading the Scriptures at home.

God has spoken on this issue; his Word explicitly says:

Let us not give up meeting together, as some are in the habit of doing, but let us encourage one another—and all the more as you see the Day approaching (Heb. 10:25).

This is his Word, and no one can neglect the gathering together with God's people and at the same time obediently live the Christian life.

One may say, "I already know everything they are going to say, so why should I attend?" Let me ask, if you already know what is going to be preached, how much do you practice of what you know? If people who don't have regular meals have difficulty in keeping up their strength, then how can people keep up their spiritual strength without gathering with other believers for spiritual meals?

As I said earlier, an enormous problem confronts modern society—the problem of homelessness. A similar problem confronts the Christian community—the problem of untold numbers of believers who are spiritually homeless. They have no family caring for them, and they are not involved in caring for others.

THE TESTIMONY OF THE MARTYRS

Listen to the testimony of the persecuted Church throughout the world. It is reported that more than 200 million Christians throughout the world live in daily fear of secret police, vigilantes, or state repression and discrimination. Today's martyrdom parallels the severest times in Church history. The challenging thing about their testimony is that many of them are persecuted simply because they refuse to cease gathering with their fellow believers.

This stands in stark contrast to multitudes who don't value the gathering of believers enough to meet regularly with a spiritual family, although they might show up for some special day or entertainment. One Catholic priest friend of mine said of his parishioners, "They only attend three times: for hatching, matching, and dispatching."

In light of the examples of the persecuted Christians, how can we, or anyone, take lightly the gathering together of God's people for worship and mutual edification? God loves the Church, our churches. It isn't simply anybody anywhere, but some people somewhere. The Psalmist loved

God's dwelling place as symbolized by the tabernacle in Jerusalem:

> *How lovely is your dwelling place, O Lord Almighty!*
> *My soul yearns, even faints for the courts of the Lord;*
> *my heart and my flesh cry out for the living God.*
> *Even the sparrow has found a home, and the swallow*
> *a nest for herself, where she may lay her young—a*
> *place near your altar, O Lord Almighty, my King and*
> *my God* (Ps. 84:1-3).

We may object, noting the lack of spirituality in this or that congregation, but God recognized the Corinthian congregation, saying, *"Don't you know that you yourselves are God's temple and that God's Spirit lives in you"* (1 Cor. 3:16). If we think he is speaking only of us as individuals, note that the Greek word for "you" here is a plural "you," meaning that he dwells in us as a body of people, his temple. And this concept is confirmed by a number of other passages of Scripture.

Aren't pride and the deception of self-sufficiency behind the persuasion that one doesn't need to gather with a spiritual family? Why else do some say, *"I do not belong to the body"* or *"I don't need you"* (1 Cor. 12:15,21)? Or, those who *"seem to be weaker are indispensable"* (1 Cor. 12:22). What is the worth of a hand if severed from the body? Does not "nature" teach us our need for each other? Isn't it our self-centeredness (our dislikes of style and personality) that seeks to rationalize non-attendance? Doesn't this nibble on the fringes of self-idolatry?

You are important! Others may feel so unimportant and inconsequential that they believe it makes no difference whether they attend or not. But the Scriptures teach that we should have *"equal concern for each other"* (1 Cor. 12:25). No child of God is unimportant.

Church is home—the sharing of a meal, a place of brothering one another, a refuge where we experience love, acceptance, and forgiveness. It is a place where we identify with each other and don't have to gain acceptance by achievement in the workplace.

C.S. LEWIS COMMENTS,

When I first became a Christian, about fourteen years ago, I thought that I could do it on my own, by retiring to my rooms and reading theology, and I wouldn't go to the churches and Gospel Halls.... I dislike very much their hymns, which I considered fifth-rate poems set to sixth-rate music. But as I went on I saw great merit in it. I came up against different people of quite different outlooks and different education, and then gradually my conceit just began peeling off. I realized that the hymns (which were just sixth-rate music) were nevertheless being sung with devotion and benefit by an old saint in elastic-side boots in the opposite pew, and then you realize you aren't fit to clean those boots. It gets you out of your solitary conceit.[4]

∾ NOTES

[1] Lewis. *Caring For People God's Way*, as quoted by the American Association of Christian Counselors.

[2] Merton. *No Man is an Island*

[3] Packer. *Truth & Power*. 75.

[4] Lewis. *God in the Dock*. 61,62.

CHAPTER NINE

THE NEW TESTAMENT MEETING

How does such a meeting differ from all other meetings? What is the purpose of this meeting? Does the gathering of a few Christians in a coffee shop constitute a church? Can you tell the difference when you have attended a church meeting?

HOW DOES A NORMAL NEW TESTAMENT CHURCH GATHERING FUNCTION?

We meet to draw near to God and to one another. In drawing near to God we come to worship, and the issue is not what we get out of the gathering but rather the glory we give to him. We draw near to one another to build one another up in the understanding of God's Word (1 Cor. 14:12) and to encourage one another to walk in the light of God's Word (Heb. 10:24).

To "edify" is to build as when one builds a home. Picture this: If every one of us brought a board or brick to contribute to an edifice and if we spent time each time we came placing this into a needed part of a building, in a short time a building would arise where there was none, or if there was, the building would rapidly increase in size. Or consider the opposite: If everyone came empty handed but took a board or a brick away from the building each time they left, it would not take long to remove a building. Now think of this analogy when we attend the gathering of God's people and hear Paul's admonishing, *"...try to excel in gifts that build up the church"* (1 Cor. 14:12).

I would like to affirm the primacy of reading, preaching, and teaching the Word of God for the building up of God's people. Making God's Word and the sacrament (visual word) the centerpiece of the gathering of believers is absolutely imperative. Not only is this the teaching of Scripture but it is also the witness of history.

When we understand the NT's teaching about the NT meeting, we will prepare our hearts for service, and we will gather with an expectant faith unto him with a sense of awe and adoration. We will be motivated to contribute to the spiritual growth of the body of people as well as to various individuals.

Consider how the people of God in the OT prepared themselves for drawing near to God. Think of how important it was to be washed and clean. The church meeting begins a long time before the service starts. Often we neglect to prepare our hearts for a corporate encounter with God.

One of the reasons this chapter is included is that for churches to maintain their identity, integrity, and credibility, it is essential that our gatherings glorify God and edify people. And it is important that Christians not be perceived as being *"out of* [their] *mind"* (1 Cor. 14:23). Otherwise they will be written off by those whom they are sent to evangelize. The validity of a meeting depends on the "product"—the truth dispensed.

WHEN ALL ELSE FAILS, READ THE INSTRUCTIONS.

Just as God left specific instructions for worship in the Old Testament, so the New Testament comprehends and lays down principles that govern the NT meeting.

The Church is under the headship of Jesus Christ, which means that everything is under his Word. J. I. Packer said:

> Now it is the nature of the church to live under the authority of Jesus Christ as its teacher no less than as its king and its priest.

Thus, as we discussed before, "Sola Scriptura" applies to the NT meeting.

Today, the Scriptures are under attack on at least three sides:

1. *the authority and veracity of Scriptures by liberals;*

2. *the sufficiency of Scripture by the addition of tradition to Scripture;*

3. *the closed canon by adding "prophecies," thus making the Bible an open-ended book.*

The Word and the Spirit are one. God doesn't speak with a forked tongue. The Spirit and the Word are like Siamese twins—inseparable. We do not find the one without the other. Many today act as though they are free to do whatever seems to work, without reference to any scriptural principle. The Church is the Lord's Church, and we cannot afford to go beyond Scripture.

Some key passages relevant to the NT meeting are:

1. **Matthew 18:15-20** *(prayer is the primary function mentioned);*

2. **Hebrews 10** *(the gathering is compared to the gathering in the OT temple, emphasizing "drawing near" to God as well as for mutual encouragement);*

3. **1 Timothy 2-3:16** *(primarily the pattern here is that found in the Jewish synagogue with the emphasis on prayer, the reading of Scripture, and worship);*

4. **1 Corinthians 11-14** *(centering on the Communion, with regulations for the NT meeting, with special mention of the "gifts," and with particular proscriptions relating to prophecies and speaking in tongues).*

The latter details the principles of the NT meeting.

HOW COMPREHENSIVE ARE THESE GUIDING PRINCIPLES? READ THE TEXTS AND JUDGE FOR YOURSELF.

The principles set forth in 1 Corinthians 12-14 appear to be very comprehensive. Consider the all-inclusive language: *"no one"* (12:3); *"in all"* (6); *"common good"* (7); *"All these"* (11); *"the body"* (12, 13); *"we were all"* (12, 13); *"the whole body"* (17); *"anyone"* (14:2); *"everyone"* (3); *"the church"* (4,5); *"will anyone"* (7); *"How can one"* (16); *"the other man"* (17); *"all of you"* (18); *"the whole church"* (23); and *"some unbelievers"* (23,24). The series of principles is plainly comprehensive and doesn't allow for an open-ended approach, allowing one to add or take away from these as one might "feel led."

It is evident that some of the functions of the gifts of the Spirit described in these chapters are more suited to small-group meetings in one of the house churches. Physical limitations such as time, space, and audibility dictate such a conclusion. All of a large congregation cannot be edified when they cannot even hear.

The fourteen guiding principles that I have identified are:

1. Who is in attendance?

The Lord Jesus, the whole church, the uninitiated, and the unbeliever. Who is in attendance regulates what happens in the meeting, a fact that should be obvious but which sometimes escapes some of us. Paul shows how we need to be sensitive to who is attending a meeting (1 Cor. 14:23).

2. Jesus is Lord.

All are under his sovereignty. He gives gifts as he wills. He chooses when to manifest himself. We must not initiate or imitate spiritual manifestations. Consider the consequences when Israel yielded to the "temptation in the wilderness" when God had chosen not to manifest his supernatural power (Heb. 3:8; 1 Cor. 10:1-13). His Lordship is reflected by our obedience to his Word.

3. The "same Spirit" with different "manifestations" is emphasized (12:4).

The "fingerprint" of God is evident by differences of manifestation, much like the variety seen in flowers and snowflakes.

4. The gifts of the Spirit are supernatural, though their manifestations often seem very natural.

I call it supernaturally natural. When people seek to manifest something supernatural, one can almost be certain that it is counterfeit. The gifts are manifestations of the Spirit, not merely enhanced human abilities or talent. They are the Lord's abilities made visible by his body.

I do not want to imply that the NT meeting is the only place or even the primary place where the gifts of the Spirit are to be exercised. Look at the life of our Lord and at the times when his powers (gifts, if you will) were manifested, and you will be convinced that the gathering is certainly not the only place for spiritual gifts.

5. Each individual is important.

No one is dispensable because an individual doesn't fit into our program (12:22,25,27). However, this does not mean an individual can take over a meeting.

6. The gifts of the Spirit function within the context of God-appointed leadership (1 Cor. 12:27,28; 1 Thess. 5:12,19).

One of these words describing this leadership ("administration" in NIV) comes from a Greek word used at times for a ship's pilot. (See Acts 27:11—"the pilot.") People who foster meetings without oversight foster shipwrecks. "Gifted" people who reject oversight are to be rejected themselves for they do not exhibit the Spirit as described by James, who says a spiritually wise man should be, *"Easy to be entreated"* (Jas. 3:17,18 KJV) ["ready to be persuaded," Gk.].

Leaders are often perceived as quenching the Spirit when they are only exercising their God-given gift of leadership and oversight. If we truly believe God is manifesting himself through a gift of the Spirit, we should give time to understand, evaluate, and apply those words we believe to be from God. When we treat lightly such manifestations, we confess we don't actually consider them authentic words of prophecy. Such light treatment could not be more opposite to the Scripture: *"...So he will fall down and worship God, exclaiming, 'God is really among you'"* (1 Cor. 14:25).

If we forfeit a leader's oversight, we forfeit the divine protection God has provided.

7. Love is the supreme controlling motive (1 Cor. 13).

Love for God's people motivates us to seek and yield ourselves to God in order to meet needs. Love is sensitive to others and accordingly regulates how gifts are manifested (1 Cor. 13:4-6). Love provides a non-critical attitude in which spiritual gifts may flourish, the kind of climate in which participation is most acceptable.

8. The edification of the body of believers is the focus of love.

The church meeting is for the edification of all (14:4, 12). Private things aren't for public meetings. In this light, we need to examine much public speaking in tongues which has become a part of a "sacred" tradition amongst some Pentecostal/Charismatic people.

9. Everything in these chapters assumes that believers are in self-control.

It is pointless for Paul to write these things unless we have sufficient self-control to obey these Scriptures. Self-control is a gift from God, for the fruit of the Spirit is self-control (Gal. 5:23). *"The spirits of the prophets are subject to the control of the prophets"* (1 Cor. 14:32). People who encourage meetings to be out of control, supposedly under the control of the Spirit, are plainly not conforming to God's Word. And the rule that guides some, "I never thought of this before; therefore, it must be God," must not govern our meetings. If it is of God, the revelation will not vanish into thin air. Revelations from God will abide as they did on the prophets who called it, "the burden of the Lord."

10. There is an evangelistic purpose in the NT meeting.

Hence Paul's concern for what happens when the unconverted are present (14:15,16). This suggests that some meetings may be designed for a specific purpose, such as evangelism, teaching, prayer, fellowship, etc.

11. "But everything should be done in a fitting and orderly way" (1 Cor. 14:40).

This statement concludes a section that, in my understanding, begins with 1 Cor. 11:3. Therefore, it is the controlling principle regulating all that happens in relationship to dress, how the Lord's Table is observed, and waiting for others to partake of Communion. It is also sensitive to social customs and culture, hence some of the instructions found in 1 Cor. 11-14 are not found elsewhere in the NT.

W. H. Marsh sees "decently" as an established way to conduct services, particularly Communion services, of which he says, "Apostolic churches were not at liberty to make of the Lord's Supper whatever they pleased."[1] Then he cites Liddell and Scott's lexicon for a definition of "decently," which is "well formed, hence, symmetrical, adapted to attract and make a favorable impression on the spectator."

Some have countered this reasoning by saying that there is a difference between God's order and man's. However, the point of reference is not God but the person coming into the service (14:24). And this is why the passage also includes some local customs that relate to women which are not mentioned in other passages of Scripture.

12. What is said or done in a meeting in the name of God must reflect the character of God and not leave those in attendance in a state of confusion.

The beauty and harmony we see in God's creation should find some counterpart in our services. Some people don't seem to think they have had a great meeting unless there is an earthquake or a violent storm. Earthquakes and storms intersperse the NT record but they were not the order.

13. Balance is required.

The meeting must not be given over to manifestations of the gifts of the Spirit. Prophetic messages and speaking in tongues are limited by number lest they take over a meeting (14:27-31). (If you have "been there," you know what I am writing about.) The balance I am speaking of is the kind of balance you find in your own physical body where the muscles in counter-tension make it possible to stand erect. This makes no room for individuals who take over a meeting, diverting attention from Christ and his Word to focus on themselves.

14. The church service is one of participation and not merely one of observation (14:26).

A purpose in many liturgies is to involve the congregation in participation. When some speak and write against liturgies, they need to compare the content of some liturgies with some of the empty words for which divine inspiration is claimed.

Ponder Paul's exhortation:

Let the peace of Christ rule in your hearts, since as members of one body you were called to peace. And be thankful. Let the word of Christ dwell in you richly as you teach and admonish one another with all wisdom, and as you sing psalms, hymns and spiritual songs with gratitude in your hearts to God (Col. 3:15,16).

Many scholars believe this passage is talking about a church service. It is significant in this connection that there be an "abundance" (rich indwelling) of the Word of God.

This vision of the body's members ministering to each other is indeed exciting and challenging. However, part of the purpose for the NT meeting was to equip the people of God to function as Jesus' Church on Monday as well as on Sunday. The Church has a responsibility to see that its members reach their maximum potential. Let us, then, take what we have gained in our church gathering into our daily lives—the strength, power, presence, and guidance of our Lord as well as the fellowship, caring, and support of our brothers and sisters in Christ.

∾ NOTES

[1] Marsh. *The New Testament Church.* 234.

CHAPTER TEN

THE PASTOR—LEADER OF THE LEADERS

May the Lord, the God of spirits of all mankind, appoint a man over this community to go out and come in before them, one who will lead them out and bring them in, so the Lord's people will not be like sheep without a shepherd [pastor] (Num. 27:15-17).

HOW CAN WE BECOME A MORE EFFECTIVE TEAM? HOW CAN WE BE MORE LIKE OUR LORD?

The form or pattern of the New Testament Church is a body of people led by a leader. Pastors are called to be the leaders of a local congregation even though they may have some other title. Without leadership, we cannot function as a normal NT church. These affirmations are supported throughout this chapter.

THE EXAMPLE OF PETER

"Then Peter stood up with the Eleven, raised his voice and addressed the crowd..." (Acts 2:14). The Day of Pentecost was a high-water mark in the life of God's people. Some things were peculiar to that day, but the pattern of leader-

ship is the only aspect I want to draw to your attention.

Peter, newly restored after denying his Lord, stood as the premier spokesman. He was flanked by eleven other apostles, but he alone spoke. These same men were only recently concerned as to who would be in a position of leadership in Christ's kingdom. Now they stood as one man in supportive unity. They weren't there to control Peter, nor even to form a committee of checks and balances. What Peter said was beyond anything they had yet confessed or understood. Nevertheless, they were in solid support of the spokesman.

The message had a mighty impact on the audience. Have we sufficiently considered the potential of a team united behind a leader?

THE SCRIPTURAL PATTERN

Leaders have a leader.

My purpose in this chapter is to show that leaders of churches, according to Scripture, are led by a leader of leaders, usually called the pastor. This pattern, in my understanding, most accurately reflects the divine order and best shows forth the glory of God.

When God has a plan he appoints a man to implement that plan. He chose Abraham, Moses, and David to lead his people. Further, God gave them judges when people cried out to the Lord for deliverance. These judges united the people in saving action. When there was no leader, *"everyone did as he saw fit"* (Judg. 21:25) and the enemy ravaged God's people. Likewise, we read in the book of Acts of how men led in the proclamation of the gospel and in the planting of churches. And the story is the same in the epistles. (The book of Judges brings out three very important and relevant issues: 1) the power of prayer, for when they cried out to God; 2) the importance of a leader, for when there was no leader, everyone just did his own thing; and 3) the significance of one individual, for the tide was turned again and again by just one person.)

In contrast, some have proposed a leadership of God's churches by leaderless committees commonly made up of men called elders, deacons or trustees. (Titles are not the issue, but rather leadership and function.)

Leaders must be empowered...

whether they are lay leaders, or are called elders or deacons, or if they have no title at all. They form an invaluable team. Without such, not much has or will ever be accomplished. These leaders must have delegated power to fulfill their office, but this empowerment is not independent of *their* leaders. They are an extension of the leader and, therefore, multiply his effectiveness. They lead others into following by following themselves. They share in the vision, and their creative input is God's means of filling out the leadership of his Church. Their prayer, sacrificial giving, and loving care make the wheels turn. Their presence and words of encouragement have sustained many pastors through difficult days. Together they serve our Lord and his people.

Before you jump to a wrong conclusion...

I am certain that there is no scriptural basis for autocratic, imperialistic, or dictatorial leadership. The NT provides no foundation for a leader who does not listen to his team of leaders or to the congregation as a whole, since it is the final court of appeal (Matt. 18:17). Leaders who listen to no one and expect their team of leaders to simply rubber-stamp whatever they do violate the command not to "lord it" over God's people. Our Lord taught "servant leadership" both by precept and by example.

In addition, Paul gave a very specific direction in 1 Tim. 3:3 when he used the word "gentle" in his list of qualifications for an elder. Its meaning excludes the authoritarian leader, for the word means to "listen with sweet reasonableness." (This definition is a summary of my own word study.) Vine suggests, "gentleness, long-suffering, patience...."[1] Therefore, we can see from Scripture what is expected of leaders.

Titles

Elder, pastor, and bishop are used almost synonymously in Acts 20, Titus 1 and 1 Peter 5. "Elder" describes the *person*, "pastor" describes the *work* (almost without an exception it is an active verb and not a noun), and "bishop" describes the *office*. However, the term "bishop" carries a specific meaning indicating a role or office. Vine defines it as "an overseer"[2] and *The Analytical Greek Lexicon* as "an inspector, overseer; a watcher, guardian."[3] It is used in 1 Peter 5:2 to describe one taking oversight.

An Incorrect Presumption

To say that the plural use of "elder" indicates that there was no leader of the leaders is an incorrect interpretation. While many emphasize the plural use of "elders" in the NT, they fail to note that the things pertaining to a bishop are singular in 1 Timothy 3. We read into the plural use of "elder" something that is not necessarily there. Compare other uses of the plural: senators, policemen, etc.

Each of these groups has a leader.

According to *The Greek English Lexicon of the New Testament*, "elder" is used for "civic as well as religious officials... members of local councils... the Sanhedrin."[4] Each of these groups of leaders had a leader of leaders amongst them, and in no case does the plural use in these cases suggest there was not a leader of the leaders. Unless one can demonstrate that plural usage proves there is no leader of the leaders, it is irrelevant to the argument for a leaderless group of elders. Remember that the synagogue, after which much in the NT Church is patterned, had a *"ruler of the synagogue"* (Mark 5:35 KJV).

Two passages of Scripture are often cited in the discussion of plural elders within one congregation. They are 1 Peter 5 and Acts 20. Although I am not contending that churches should not have more than one elder, it is plain that these two passages are not sufficient proof to conclude that Peter is talking about plural elder leadership in one congregation. The epistle of 1 Peter tells us in the introduction that the letter was written to Pontus, Galatia, Cappadocia, Asia, and Bithynia. Hence, it is obvious that there are many congregations even though the believers are all called one "flock."

The passage in Acts 20 parallels 1 Peter 5. I believe the elders came from a number of different house-churches. One of these house-churches is identified in 1 Corinthians 16:19.[5] The "houses" Paul visited (Acts 20:20) were apparently "house-churches," and the elders in this passage probably came from the various house-churches. Some reasons for this conclusion are:

- *the ministry of Paul, Apollos, Aquila, and Priscilla over many years would not have resulted in only one congregation;*

- *the success of the gospel had to be so extensive as to threaten the trade of the idol makers there, which resulted in strong persecution;*
- *the planting of churches throughout Asia Minor resulted from Paul's extended time in Ephesus;*
- *churches, which at this point in Church history met in houses, were limited in size;*
- *An example of multiple house-churches in one city is seen in Romans 16, where we are able to identify a number of house-churches.*

BIBLICAL BASIS FOR CONCLUDING THE SINGULAR MEANING OF "BISHOP"

An interesting way of dealing with the office of elder is suggested by the various translations.

Translations of Key Passage

Different translations consistently call a bishop an "office-holder." First Timothy 3 is thus translated by the most competent Greek scholars: *"If any one aspires the office of a Bishop…"* (KJV); *"If any man aspires to the office of overseer…"* (NASB)[6]; *"If any one seeketh for the office of a bishop…"* (ASV)[7]; *"When a man aspires to be a Presiding Officer in the Church…"* (TCNT)[8]; *"If any one desires the "office of superintendent…"* (GSPD)[9]; *"the office of a minister…"* (Mon); *"the office of a pastor…"* (BER)[10]; and, *"If a man desires the position of a bishop, he desires a good work"* (NKJV). (The grammar of this passage must be the basis of the consistency of translation since there is no word for "office" in the original text.)

Singular and Plural in 1 Timothy 3

The grammar of this chapter is very significant. When speaking of a bishop, ten verbs are singular in contrast with seven plural verbs describing the role of deacons. Walter Lock tells us that this contrast of singular and plural verbs cannot be ignored when interpreting this passage.[11] Also note that the word "bishop" is with a definite article and the word "deacons" does not have an article, so it should be rendered, "the bishop." This is not to suggest that there is an ecclesiastical hierarchy (which came later in Church history), but only to say that there was a leader of the leaders.

QUALIFICATIONS

Paul gives us the qualifications of an elder in 1 Timothy 3. One of these qualifications stands out as it bears on our subject, and that is: *"He must manage his own family well…. If anyone does not manage his own family, how can he take care of God's church?"* (1 Tim. 3:4,5).

Think about the pattern of leadership implied here. A family is not under the leadership of a committee of two but of one (1 Cor. 11:3). If there were ever a place where there would be committee leadership it would be the family, and the committee would be husband and wife.

However, Scripture again gives us the answer in the following: *"Does not nature itself teach us…"* (1 Cor. 11:14 WMS[12]). Here, as well as in a number of places in the NT, there is an appeal to the inherent teaching of nature. One thing nature teaches is that all bodies throughout nature have one head. And it is evident that having a head in heaven does not exclude having a head on earth.

Now I want you to realize that the head of every man

is Christ, and the head of the woman is man, and the head of Christ is God (1 Cor. 11:3).

When Christ is the head of the family, his headship makes the husband the head of the home. Christ, being the head of the Church, does not exclude a pastor from being the leader of a local church, rather Christ's headship is the very basis of the pastor's leadership of the leaders.

Peter teaches the concept of a senior elder/pastor in 1 Peter 5:1-9 when he addresses the elders. Peter speaks as an elder to the elders. Peter himself, in fact, is a leader of the leaders and is performing this role here. He does not address them as an apostle but as an elder. The subject is elders. Within this category, he addresses "younger" elders. If this simply described younger men, it would have been in one of the earlier categories in this letter, i.e., citizens (2:13); slaves (2:18); wives (3:1); husbands (3:7); *"finally, all of you"* (3:8). Hence, we are not reverting to the social category of young men but rather of younger "elders" which is the group addressed in 1 Peter 5. Thus, this is a basis for a senior pastor/elder. This explanation follows that suggested by Kuhl, Weiss, Schott, Bruckner in *The New International Critical Commentary St. Peter and St. Jude*.[13]

TIMOTHY

Timothy's "job description," as seen by the commands given to him, is the job description of a pastor and not just a special "one time only" delegate of an apostle. He had oversight of those teaching (1 Tim. 1:3). He was to oppose false teachers and false teaching (1:18,19). He had oversight of a public meeting (2:1-12). He had oversight of those being chosen for officers in the local church (1 Tim. 3). He possessed authority with regard to teaching (4:11). He was a public reader of Scripture and a teacher and a preacher (4:13). He had oversight of church affairs (5:17-20). He was a mentor of forthcoming teachers (2 Tim. 2:2). His primary work was in relationship to the Word of God (2 Tim. 2:15). Recurring and dominant words describing his responsibility had to do with "teaching and preaching" (4:2-4).

THE GODHEAD—THE SUPREME EXAMPLE

The Godhead is led by the Father. There is complete equality among members of the Trinity. The Father, however, is the leader of the Trinity. The Son speaks only what he hears his Father say (John 5:19,20). The Holy Spirit does not initiate anything himself. He *"will not speak on his own; he will only speak what he hears…"* (John 16:13). Equality does not suggest that one is not the leader. This is the pattern we see in the Godhead. The Trinity is not a committee without a leader. All are subject to the Father (1 Cor. 15:24-28). The Church reflects the very nature of God, the fellowship within the Godhead, and the structure as seen in this Corinthian passage.

JESUS, THE GOD-MAN

Jesus modeled the principle of leading by serving. He humbly stooped to wash the disciples' feet. In doing so, he didn't abdicate his role of leadership; rather, he led them into servanthood. The problem the disciples had that day was that no one was willing to step forward and be a servant leader.

Jesus is the epitome of his own teaching. We follow him. He was and is the leader of leaders. He didn't give us a pattern of a leaderless group.

Jesus' example of a true shepherd/pastor was a person

who would lay down his life for the sheep. It separates true shepherds from hirelings. So I am not talking about authoritarian leadership but about leaders who are ready to lay down their lives day after day for the flock of God.

Jesus' words about leadership, according to some, exclude the idea of someone being a leader or person in charge. Scripture does *not* support this conclusion. Consider Matthew 23:8-12. It begins by speaking of brothers (a group of equals). But it does not exclude the idea of someone becoming a leader. It just explains how that leadership would be attained, i.e., through humility and sacrificial service. If this passage excludes someone as a leader of the leaders, it logically follows that it excludes all leadership, including elders and deacons. All of us are called to servanthood and are to be led by those persons who best model humility and servanthood. Servanthood doesn't exclude leadership. Spiritual leaders serve by leading and lead by serving. And anyone who knows anything about their culture knows that families of brothers had a leader amongst them.

The main point in the Matthew passage is the *"one Teacher, the Christ,"* the head of the Church. All must be in subjection to him. What he teaches must overrule all else. And if he has called and delegated someone to a task, then to fail to receive his delegated leader is a rejection of the Lord who appointed him. Jesus' words in no way restrained Peter from being the primary leader for the first twelve chapters of Acts.

Jesus' teaching about shepherds (pastors) gives us the pattern for shepherding sheep. The shepherd *"goes to the lost sheep"* (Matt. 10:6), restores the sheep that has fallen into the pit (Matt. 12:11), and seeks the sheep that has wandered off (Matt. 18:12-13).

The Greek word for "ruling" God's flock is not a political word but a shepherding word. Teaching is the primary way in which God's shepherds rule his flocks. *"Remember them which have the rule over you"* (KJV), *"who have spoken unto you the word of God"* (Heb. 13:7).

> *Obey* [be persuaded by—Gk.] *your leaders and submit* [yield—Gk.] *to their authority. They keep watch over you as men who must give an account. Obey them so that their work will be a joy, not a burden, for that would be of no advantage to you* (Heb. 13:17).

Therein is a formula to bring God praise, leaders joy, and the congregation blessing.

THE APOSTLES

Jesus' apostles were leaders of the leaders. When the "chips were down," Paul didn't hesitate to lead, even when Peter was not in accord (Gal. 2:14). In the reading of the NT one finds many lists of leaders, and it is rather easy to identify the leader of the leaders in many of these lists. A specific case is in Acts 15:36-41. This list includes Paul, Barnabas, Mark, and Silas. The disagreement amongst them brought out who was the leader of these leaders, and this was recognized by the others. When the disagreement concluded, Paul, the leader, and those with him, were the only people *"commended by the brothers"* (15:40). Where did anyone get the idea of government by consensus?

JAMES

James was the pastor of the church in Jerusalem, as the evidence shows: *"When they finished, James spoke up..."* (Acts 15:13); *"It is my judgment..."* (Acts 15:19); *"Tell James..."* (Acts 12:17); *"The next day Paul and the rest of us went to see James, and all the elders were present"* (Acts 21:18); *"Then he* (Jesus) *appeared to James, then to all the apostles"* (1 Cor. 15:7); *"I saw none of the other apostles— only James, the Lord's brother"* (Gal. 1:19); *"James, Peter and John, those reputed to be pillars…"* (Gal. 2:9) [observe who is mentioned first]; *"Before certain men came from James"* (Gal. 2:12).

DELEGATES

Pastors are delegates of Christ and the apostles.

All leadership is delegated. No one but the Lord has inherent authority. The call of God is how God delegates us to our specific roles. That call is recognized and confirmed by a local church. The essence of organization is delegation.

When the mother of James and John sought Jesus' favor so that he might delegate her sons to positions of power, Jesus said that such appointments are in the Father's hand. Further, he pointed out that such a role will come at a great cost to those delegated to such leadership. He did not say there would not be leaders but rather told how leadership would be attained.

When God calls or delegates individuals to a task, God gifts them for that task. People who are called need to wait on God for empowering gifts. They need to prepare for the work to which God has called them. The functions of the body of Christ are divided up according to the gifts God has given. Thus, the Church's delegation of individuals is simply a confirmation of what God has already done. Congregations need to be more sensitive to the callings and gifts of God.

Jack Hayford reports:

Three years ago, I invited pastors across the nation to write me and describe as well as they could, "The reason I'm in the ministry." It was no surprise to read the answer, "I was called of God."[14]

On a pastor's call, Eugene Peterson writes:

What I object to most is the appalling and systematic trivializing of the pastoral office. It is a part of a greater trivialization, that of the culture itself, a trivialization that is so vast and epidemic that there are days when its ruin seems assured.[15]

The sense of "call" explains the fact that in the United States alone more than a half million such dedicated servants labor tirelessly, serving humanity in the name of God. Most will agree that such a call must be confirmed. God's people need to come to grips with the reality of a God-called man serving in their midst and relate to such a person accordingly. In keeping with this concept, Hayford writes:

The center of gravity is not the stadium, but the sanctuary; not to rally around a renowned speaker, but to stand with the local pastor.[16]

George Barna quotes Bill Hybels as saying:

...three things are required from every staff member at a church: godliness, competency in the person's area and loyalty to the senior leader.[17]

In the same book he writes to pastors:

If God has called you to lead, let nothing stand in the way of the privilege you have to serve Him and to serve

129

His people through applying the gift, the resources and the opportunity He has provided to you.[18]

What is leadership? According to Bruce and Marshall Shelley, it is "the ability to influence other people."[19] They identify this as "power," not coercion through threat and punishment but persuasion. They describe such as transformational leaders whose leadership starts with vision. People who can successfully communicate their vision to others are, in fact, leaders.

Leaders affect change, and they must expect resistance to change. In relationship to churches, "People need to know what the church is about and what it is trying to do."[20] In the process of change we expect conflict. Don't expect to lead if you can't stand the heat of the kitchen.

ANGELS ON ASSIGNMENT

The pastors of the churches in Revelation 2 and 3 are called angels. When the apostle John was told to write letters to the churches, he wrote, *"To the angel of the church in..."* (Rev. 2:1). Each church had an angel. The Greek word for "angel" essentially means "messenger." It is used in the Septuagint translation of the OT with regard to Malachi, to a priest and the prophesied messenger of the covenant. (The Septuagint was in wide use at the time the NT was written and is quoted many times therein.)

It is virtually impossible to apply "angels" in these chapters to heavenly beings. God certainly did not have a communication problem in heaven, thus needing John to write letters for him to angelic beings. The evident understanding of these "angels" is that they are the pastors of these churches. (Quite a few of us who are pastors would be delighted if heavenly beings would assume our responsibilities.)

J. A. Seiss puts it even more strongly:

> The seven stars are the angels [ministers] of the seven Churches, and as such, they are distinct from the candlesticks. Christ walks among the candlesticks, but he holds these ministers in his right hand.... Ministers have relations to Christ and to the Church, which ordinary Church members have not.[21]

Of this he continues:

> This is a doctrine from which, indeed, many deplorable abuses have sprung... and on account of which some have rejected it as not of God.... It is not a lordship; not a service to be commanded of man, but of God.[22]

If we conclude that these are angelic beings, as some think, then we have here the basis of angelic mediators between God and his Church, a characteristic of some cults.

JOB DESCRIPTIONS

Bishop

A bishop's job description is implied by the words used, suggests Walter Lock.[23] The job descriptions, Lock feels, are implied by the following anglicized forms of the Greek words: *episcopos*—"one leading the worship"; *proistashai*—"one presiding and standing before"; *epimelasetai*—"take care of or discipline"; *didaktikon*—"teach"; *aphilarguron*—"overseeing finances"; and *philoxenon*—"representing the Christian community to the outside world."

Man of God

The title "man of God" given to Timothy lifts his role to a high level. Paul writes, *"But you, man of God..."* (1 Tim. 6:11). When Paul uses

> "an appellation for Timothy as a minister of the Word of God":
> ...the background for the term is in the OT where in each case it refers to one of God's servants or agents: Moses, or one of the prophets.[24]

Fellow-Servant

Servant leadership is the dividing line between the NT pattern of leadership and patterns of leadership devised by various religious organizations. Some have taken the passages on this subject and sought to eliminate the concept of a leader of the leaders. The following study demonstrates that this is not true.

John Stott describes a servant by using a number of challenging words from the Greek text of the NT.[25] Some of these words translate as follows:

- *"household steward,"* which is used to describe "a manager of a household or of household affairs";

- *"herald"* means "...one who stands between a sovereign and his people and who possesses a more direct authority to represent his master";

- a word meaning a *"bond slave"*—one "who has no legal rights and belongs to his master as a personal possession";

- a word meaning *"a household servant,"* or sometimes *"one who rowed in the lower tier of a war galley"*;

- the word from which we get "*deacon*," but which is used in an untechnical way to describe all kinds of service including "what we would call an ordained minister."

As one can see, there is nothing in these words to indicate that there is no leader of the leaders.

SMITTEN SHEPHERDS AND SCATTERED SHEEP

Pastors are being smitten and sheep are being scattered. H. B. London once wrote:

I read that in a major denomination (to remain nameless) last year, twenty-five hundred pastors were forced to resign. This represented nearly seven percent of their churches. I would almost guarantee that a major portion of those resignations came because of change, and the cost was never really determined until the pastor became the sacrificial lamb.

Jesus drew his words about shepherds from the OT and the evident principle from shepherds and sheep. It was never more evident than when Jesus was stricken (Matt. 26:31).

The principle, however, is not limited to Christ. It is Satan's strategy to strike the shepherd and scatter the sheep. Often good people assist him. Tragically, it spells itself out in the lives of thousands of God's sheep who are not gathered in any flock on the Lord's Day. God's people are scattered, and one of the major reasons is that shepherds continue to be stricken and often in the houses of their friends. Thousands have dropped out of church as a result.

WHEN ASSISTANTS TAKE OVER

Deacons, according to the NT, are assistants to the elders. Deacons sometimes assume that all the material things are in their exclusive domain and tend to dominate churches by dollars instead of by Scripture. (Pastors are also vulnerable to dollar domination.)

It shouldn't be necessary to write these paragraphs, but it is. Many churches are controlled by deacons. Deacons in Scripture were chosen to assist the apostles and later the elders. But when churches place deacons in charge of all material things, they put the deacons in control of almost everything. Thus, deacons cease to be assistants and become rulers.

Consider evangelistic campaigns, building projects, additions to the staff, salaries, missionary commitments, ministries to the poor, etc.; these all are controlled by finances. Those who were intended to be assistants become controllers because they control the funds. They rule by financial control which is quite different than ruling by the teaching of the Word of God. One doesn't have to be a pastor very long to find out that those who control the money control the church. It is a far cry from the time when the money was placed at *"the apostles' feet"* (Acts 5:2), and often things that are done are not what the congregation wishes to be done. (Many who have the title of elders are, in fact, deacons, for they are not "able to teach," and they do not have a ministry in the Word of God.)

There is an ever present danger of turning pastors into hirelings, a danger to be avoided by pastors and church leaders. No one has pastored for long before being treated as an employee who is directed by his employers. If this is the practice, it won't be long before another "employer" offers a bigger salary or better benefits. Those who want a hireling will experience our Lord's words, *"...when he sees the wolf coming, he abandons the sheep and runs away. Then the wolf attacks the flock and scatters it"* (John 10:12). Gordon Smith writes:

> ...it should be noted that the church does not employ a minister. It releases him from the need of secular employment and undertakes properly to maintain him and his family so that he may do the Lord's work....[26]

REALITIES

We must deal with practical realities and not just abstract theories. When people are in need, on whom do they call? I trust that the first person they seek is the Lord, otherwise we may turn leaders into mediators between us and God. But God has placed leaders in the church upon whom we are exhorted to call (Jas. 5:14). When people ask for prayer, to whom do they turn? Whom do they seek for counsel? If it is not from us, we are probably not elders/bishops. If we don't have any followers, we are probably not leaders. If no one is learning the Scripture from us, we aren't teachers.

Most people want a strong leader unless that leader differs from them, which really shows where the problem is.

Consider this question: Who has made a difference in your life? Is it an individual or a committee?

When the sailing ships were competing for the America Cup, a wealthy person funded a team of women to compete. The wealthy person concluded that women can work together better than men, so he organized the venture without a captain. The women later said that the main reason they failed was that they had no leader.

135

Some sociologists say that no leader is necessary until you are faced with accomplishing a task. The Turkish prisoners of war survived better than anyone in the Korean War, and the American soldiers failed worse than all the others. The US Army concluded that the reason for the failure was the American tendency toward individualism, which resisted submitting to a leader. The Turks, on the other hand, united behind a leader, and if the leader was killed, they immediately elected another one.

ACCEPT THE LEADERS.

We need to learn how to accept a leader of leaders. Timid God-appointed leaders, such as Timothy, need to be encouraged to step forward and fulfill the ministry to which God has called them. Everyone recognized for his or her accomplishments in Scripture were people who stepped forward to do the tasks God gave them. And all who have accomplished great things for God in Church history have done the same.

One of my purposes for this chapter is to show and confirm a biblical confidence to those in leadership. However, lest any reader suppose this section is a blanket endorsement of all pastors, let us remember that Paul's letters to Timothy distinguished between good and poor pastors and gave us the criteria by which we can tell the difference. There are some leaders who need to be rejected: *"Remember that for three years I never stopped warning each of you night and day with tears"* (Acts 20:31). This wasn't an evangelistic warning to sinners; it was a warning to the church at Ephesus. It warned about *"savage wolves"* who would not *"spare the flock,"* and it also warned against their own men who would *"draw away disciples after them"* (Acts 20:29,30). Some of the elder/pastors addressed in this warning were probably some of the disciplined leaders mentioned in Paul's letters to Timothy.

Today we are faced with similar problems. Leaders within a congregation start attacking the leader God has given their church. The very people who affirmed the will of God when they called their pastor subsequently reject their own guidance when they turn their backs on the same leader.

HOW TO LEAD

This is not an argument for "one-man government" but only that the pastor, as we have come to know him, is simply the leader of the leaders. If he can't delegate and empower those working with him, he cannot be a good leader. If he can't lead the leaders or lead the congregation, he is not a leader. He must not resort to "lording over" God's flock. He must lead by a life of humble sacrifice and refuse to be a hireling. He must lead by persuasion, by instruction, and by example. But he must lead!

In his leading, he must develop a strong team of leaders whom he must empower to fulfill their calling and ministry. If he is determined to have his hand in every detail, one must conclude he is called to a small church.

Human lordship is exercised when people are compelled to violate their consciences by the demands and commands of another. Lenski said:

> The church still suffers from self-appointed lords and spurious authority. It is easy to detect, for these lords either presume to dispense faith and its doing from the Word of our Lord, or they presume to add some requirements to our faith and our practice that is beyond the Word of our Lord.[27]

137

In other words, he defines "lording over God's flock" as teaching doctrines or practices not found in Scripture.

The thrust of what I have written has to do with structure of leadership, but structure does not take the place of spirituality. Churches today are in dire need of being led into true spirituality by spiritual men. "The central conclusion is that the American church is dying due to lack of strong leadership."[28]

These are times that cry out for leadership, and that in the right direction. Therefore, *"If you are a leader, exert yourself to lead"* (Rom. 12:8 NEB[29]). And for God's sake, for your church's sake, and for your own sake, lead in the right direction!

∾ NOTES

[1] Vine. *Vine's Complete Expository Dictionary*. 263.

[2] Vine. *Vine's Complete Expository Dictionary*. 67

[3] *The Analytical Greek Lexicon*.

[4] Bauer, Arndt, and Gingrich. *The Greek English Lexicon of the New Testament*. 706.

[5] See Fee's comments, *Commentary on 1 and 2 Timothy*. 8.

[6] *The New American Standard Bible*. The Lockman Foundation, 1963.

[7] *The American Standard Version*

[8] *The Twentieth Century New Testament*. Moody Bible Institute.

[9] *The New Testament: An American Translation*. Edgar Goodspeed. University of Chicago, 1948.

[10] *The Berkley Version in Modern English*. Gerrit Verkuyl. Zondervan, 1945.

[11] Lock. *The International Critical Commentary*.

[12] *A Translation in the Language of the People.* Charles Williams. Moody Bible Institute. © Bruce Humphries Inc., 1937

[13] Kuhl, Weiss, Schott, Bruckner. *Critical Commentary St. Peter and St. Jude.* 190.

[14] Hayford. *Pastors of Promise.* 20-21.

[15] Petersen. *Under the Predictable Planet.*

[16] Op. cit. 61.

[17] Barna. *Leaders on Leadership.*

[18] Op. cit.

[19] Bruce Shelley and Marshall Shelley. *The Consumer Church.* 218.

[20] Op. cit. 221.

[21] Seiss. *The Apocalypse.* 41.

[22] Ibid. 69.

[23] Lock. *International Critical Commentary,* in volume on "The Pastoral Epistles." 35.

[24] Fee. *Biblical Commentary I and II Timothy, Titus.*

[25] Stott. *The Preacher's Portrait.*

[26] Smith. *Evangelical Fellowship of Congregational Churches.* 27.

[27] Lenski. *Interpretation of First and Second Corinthians.* 861, 862.

[28] Barna. Op. cit. 18.

[29] *New English Bible.* Cambridge University Press, 1961.

CHAPTER ELEVEN

THE PERSPECTIVE OF HISTORY

Nothing is more characteristic of radicalism and sectarianism than an utter want of historical sense and respect for the past. In its extreme form it rejects even the Bible as an external authority, and relies on inward inspiration.[1]

It is imperative for one to seriously look at the local church movement in light of history. "Catholics of all kinds (Roman, Eastern, Episcopal, etc.) outnumber Protestants about four to one."[2] Their claim excludes all Christians not belonging to one of these groups as well as all other forms of church government. Anglican Bishop Charles Gore declared that:

> ...the various presbyterian and congregational organizations, however venerable on many different grounds, have, in dispensing with the episcopal successions, violated a fundamental law of the Church's life....[3]

And he went on to raise the issue of "validity" that has haunted ecumenical discussions ever since, saying, "...a ministry not episcopally received is invalid...."[4]

This is not only a problem for all other Christian organizations, but it is a problem for Rome and has been a matter of study for the US bishops. So:

> Vatican II and its documents begins with the biblical concept of the Church as a pilgrim People of God rather than with the primacy of its hierarchy.[5]

They acknowledge by their teachings that they have proscribed the recognition of the Holy Spirit's work in others. (Most of the others have yet to effectively grapple with this issue).

So it is necessary to see the local church in the perspective of history and to establish its claim to being in the succession of authentic churches.

History tells us where we have been and how we got where we are, and hopefully it is useful in guiding us in the future. It helps us from repeating the mistakes of the past.

FIVE WAYS TO LOOK AT CHURCH HISTORY

Let us look together at the following five components to see how they contribute to an understanding of the local church:

1. the synagogue as the parent of the local church;

2. the primitive churches;

3. the pre-Reformation churches;

4. the Reformation churches;

5. contemporary forms of church today.

The Synagogue Model

The synagogues in the Acts appear as the nurseries of the infant Churches from which they indeed are often prematurely ejected…. Such a succession would naturally retain both the general type of worship and the official system of the body from which it parted company…. Thus we find the Christian assembly called a 'synagogue' not only in the epistle of James (2:2) and the Ebionite communities, but even in the Epistle of Ignatius to Polycarp.[6]

According to Schaff, "The term 'synagogue' [like our word church] signifies first, the congregation, then also the building where the congregation meets for public worship." Regarding organization:

Every synagogue had a president, a number of elders equal in rank, a reader and an interpreter, one or more envoys or clerks, called 'messengers' and a sexton or beadle for the humbler mechanical services. There were also deacons for the collection of alms in money and produce….[7]

He continues:

Officers of the synagogue—The synagogues were governed by the elders who were presided over by the ruler of the synagogue….[8]

W. H. H. Marsh says:

If the position is correct, then in organization and government the New Testament Church and the Jewish synagogue are essentially identical…. As used in the Septuagint these words (*ekklesia* and *sunagogue*) are essentially synonyms, as are the Hebrew words they translate.[9]

The conclusion: Each synagogue was autonomous.

The Primitive Church

The NT knows of no hierarchal offices.

> It is a fact now generally recognized by all shades of opinion, that in the language of the New Testament the same officer in the Church is called indifferently 'bishop' (episcopos) and 'elder' or 'presbyter' (presbuteros).[10]

The NT knows nothing of an elder who is an elder in more than one church or over more than one church.

Without a hierarchy, we are left with autonomous local churches.

According to Alistair McGrath, a central structure of the Christian Church did not begin until Constantine.

> The relative pluralism of an understanding of doctrine... reflected the unintegrated social structure of the Christian church period; with the advent of centralization during the Constantinian period came the idea of the church as a single institutional unity, requiring uniformity in order to preserve its newfound social function and status. [11]

The writings of Clement, Ignatius, and Polycarp "are the proper link between the Canonical Scripture and the Church Fathers who succeeded them."[12] The earliest of these is Clement, who dates back to the first century.

Lightfoot says of Clement's remarks regarding church government that:

> ...they savour of the first century. We find 'episcopos' [bishop] still used as a synonym for 'presbuteros' [elder], as it is in the NT; though in the first or second

decade of the succeeding century in the Epistles of Ignatius the two words are used to designate two distinct offices of the ministry.[13]

Of the Christian ministry in Rome I have already spoken.... Not only have we no traces of bishops, but even the very existence of Rome itself could nowhere be gathered from this letter [of Clement].[14]

Clement's letter was written approximately thirty years after Paul's letter to the Romans and was a "letter from church to church, and not from the Bishop of Rome to another church."[15]

Of Bishop Lightfoot, Philip Schaff writes:

Bishop Lightfoot begins his valuable discussion of the Christian ministry with this broad and liberal statement: 'The kingdom of Christ, not being a kingdom of this world, is not limited by the restrictions which fetter other societies, political or religious.... It displays the character, not only in acceptance of all who come to seek admission, irrespective of race or class or sex, but also in the instruction and treatment of those who are already its members.... It interposes no sacrificial tribe or class between God and man, by whose intervention God alone is reconciled and man forgiven. Each individual member holds personal communion with the Divine Head. To Him immediately he is responsible, and from him directly obtains pardon and draws strength.[16]

These are a few facts from Church history by outstanding scholars, and these scholars aren't even from a congregationalist or independent persuasion.

Pre-Reformation Stage

> The fourteenth and fifteenth centuries witnessed a widespread revival of mystical piety. Usually, this mysticism did not attack the church openly, nor was it characterized by the intense emotional exaltation that is usually called mysticism.[17]

When people believe they have experienced God in a direct and intimate way, it is difficult to get them to submit to an external human authority. Also, in this period prior to the Reformation, the seat of authority began to shift from Rome to the Scriptures, an authority which many revered.

Erasmus translated the Greek New Testament in 1516. And printing presses had now begun to provide the "authority" of the printed page. People began to attempt to return to the original sources of their faith.

Wyclif, whom it is believed was born around 1320, was an Oxford scholar in England who began to write some reformatory writings challenging both the religious and civil authorities which functioned hand in hand. His biblical studies began to make a deep impression on him. He translated the Bible into English from the Vulgate, and this translation introduced new levels of freedom.

> His conception of the Church... was different from that usual in his day; it was not the congregation of the bishop of Rome but the communion of those elected of God that formed the Church.[18]

Lollards, a name applied to the English followers of Wyclif as well as of a monastic charitable society, denied the teachings of the Roman Catholic Church, and in this they were supported by Wyclif and the university. This movement deeply stirred England for nearly a half a century.

Zwingli (1484-1531) was unusually qualified to challenge the Roman Catholic Church since he was a man of:

> …uncommon Biblical and patristic scholarship…. Being a scholar… applied himself to his books and laid deep and wide foundations…. [He] prepared sixty-five theses, not at all unlike the ninety-five theses of Luther…. In accordance with the Swiss plan that before radical measures could be taken in a canton there was to be a public debate as to their expediency…. All the clergy were invited…. As a matter of fact, there was no real debate, but only a dialogue between Zwingli and the vicar-general of Constance…. He… taught… to ask Scripture proof for doctrines…. He showed a singular reluctance to accept the consistent teachings of his Anabaptist friends…. By the end of 1524 church life in Zurich was quite different…. The convents for men and women had been abolished….[19]

He became a significant influence on what was to become the Anabaptist movement.

> *The Waldensians* were the first to return to the primitive idea of the Church…. The first theologian who opposed the Roman Catholic doctrine of the Church… was Wicliff… whom Hus followed…. He denied the papal primacy…. The next champion of Protestantism to Hus is Luther….[20]

The Reformation Period and Churches

Martin Luther—The moral decline and the commercialization of religion within the Roman Catholic Church deeply troubled Martin Luther. Add to this the sense of his own sinfulness and you set the stage for the epiphany Luther experienced in Rome when he "heard" the words, *"the just shall live by faith"* (Gal. 3:11 KJV). The Reformation had arrived in force. Luther thought he could reform the Roman Catholic Church, but that was not to be. His intention had not been to leave the Church or to lay the foundation for a new ecclesiology. But the situation required a new understanding of the Church.

Luther at first took the ground of congregational independency in his writings in the Behemian Brethren (1523) and advocated the right of a Christian congregation to all, to elect and to depose its own minister. He meant, of course, a congregation of true believers not a mixed multitude of nominal professors.

> In Luther's words, 'A layman with the Scriptures is more to be believed than pope and council without the Scriptures.'
>
> But congregations of pure Christians, capable of self-government, could not be found in Germany at that time, and are impossible in state churches where churchmanship and citizenship coincide. Luther abandoned this democratic idea after the Peasants' War and called on the arm of the government for protection against the excesses of the popular will.
>
> It was not long (1542) until Luther ventured to consecrate a bishop. Soon the congregations didn't have the power to elect their own pastors and city magistrates assumed episcopal power and appointed superintendents. State churches became the established order.[21]

At the Leipzig disputation (1517) Luther defined the Church as the Communion of Saints whose existence depended upon its possession of the Word and sacraments and not of bishop or clergy. The "power of the keys," which the true Church knew, was no exclusive class-possession, but the assurance, by means of grace that sin was forgiven, independent of the personal character of the administrator.

Luther almost crossed the line to a "regenerate church" when, as reported by some, he wrote to a friend, Nicholas Haussman:

> My intention is, in the days to come, not to admit any to communion... except such as have been interviewed and have given suitable answers as to their personal faith. The rest would be excluded.

Anabaptists

> Anabaptists were asking for a regenerate church, but were greatly impeded by fanaticism and prophetism in their midst. Menno Simons is credited with rescuing the movement from the 'perils of fanaticism.' He sought a 'complete turning from fanaticism and prophetic dreams....' There must be an exercise of discipline with the congregations.[22]

With the Reformation's rejection of the hierarchy and tradition of the Roman Catholic Church, the way was open for a return to the NT pattern of local churches. The Reformers' definition of a church, at this time, was where the true gospel is preached, where church discipline is practiced, and the sacraments are administered.

The Anabaptists were only one of many groups and denominations that would seek to lay claim to being biblical after the pattern of the New Testament. These various groupings, however, would be divided essentially between three basic kinds of religious bodies: Episcopal, Presbyterian, and Congregational.

Congregationalism (not to be confused with the denomination by this name) was first labeled such in the sixteenth century as the Puritan movement started within the Church of England. Its purpose was to purify the Church of England of what were considered to be Roman Catholic influences. This led the Puritans to separate from the Church of England. By the seventeenth century, it was a powerful political party. John Owen, the Vice-Chancellor of the University of Oxford, was thought by some to be one of the most significant theologians of this period. He studied Congregationalism with a purpose of showing that it was not based on the Bible. Instead of disproving Congregationalism, he became convinced of its scriptural accuracy and became a congregationalist himself.

The following five essential principles of Congregationalism have been recognized and practiced from the beginning of Church history (before it was called Congregationalism):

1. Jesus Christ as Lord is the head of both the Church universal and the local church. This means that his Word is the ultimate authority in every matter. Leaders or groups of leaders who function as a hierarchy over churches are usurping the powers vested only in Jesus Christ.

2. Jesus Christ is present through the Holy Spirit in the local church according to his promise, *"there am I with them"* (Matt. 18:20). The "head" of the church is attached to its body. The "head" and the "headquarters" are in the same place. It is not what we do in his absence but what we do in his presence.

3. There is only *"one mediator between God and men"* (1 Tim. 2:5). No angel, leader, religious organization, or "spiritual gift" can be allowed to interpose between the believers and their Lord.

4. Churches (local) are composed of people committed to Jesus Christ and to one another. In God's eyes, churches do not include unregenerate people. Regenerate members possess certain inalienable rights and responsibilities as the heritage of a child of God. Each one is a priest unto God. Each one is gifted by God to build up the people of God. Each one has direct access to God and is invited to come boldly to the throne of grace to find grace in time of need (not just when one has been good). The "head" of the Church is accessible to each one. The primary principle is that a true church is made up of people who have been born again, a regenerate church. (From the time of St. Augustine, people have sought to relate the NT teaching of a regenerate church to the practice of including many who were obviously not regenerate but who had been baptized into the Church. Augustine sought to reconcile this by writing of a church within the Church.)

5. Each church belongs to the family of churches on earth, which are addressed, for example, as the *"churches in Galatia"* (Gal. 1:2) or the *"churches in the province of Asia"* (Rev. 1:4), or throughout the world. No church is over or under other churches but is *"with all those everywhere who call on the name of our Lord Jesus"* (1 Cor. 1:2). There is no hierarchy over these churches. However, they did identify, associate, and confer with each other. They have no scrip-

tural right to legislate for others. We would be greatly impoverished if each church were left by itself. The councils, conferences, synods, and conventions have greatly enriched our understanding of God's Word. Teachers have profitably consulted with each other. The contribution of their interaction is a valued commentary on Scripture but they must never be treated as having the authority of Scripture.

Developments in England also need to be included because of the effects on the West. The English parliament used the opportunity when Roman Catholicism's hold on England was loosened to promote Puritanism. This leads us up to the Westminster Assembly, a group of 151 persons called upon to advise parliament on religious matters. This has been called the most significant event in the history of Christian doctrine, though I am certain that all do not share that opinion. The product of that Assembly was the famous Westminster Confession, making Presbyterianism the state church of England. This confession of faith, with which there was a general agreement of Episcopal, Presbyterian, and Congregational churches, was later reworked. A minority report supported Congregationalism as opposed to Presbyterianism. A document that resulted was the "Savoy Declaration" which favored the Congregational viewpoint; that is, the concept of local churches. Meantime, the Baptist movement, as it was then being called, was meeting in private homes. Some of these homes were equipped with concealed basement rooms for their meetings, and they were equipped with trap doors leading to these basement rooms.

This condition obtained until The Act of Toleration in 1689. The Baptist emphasis on religious liberty put them in advance of their time.... Most Baptists in early America stemmed from a British background. While earliest churches were indigenous, in time the English connection became clearer.[23]

America is indebted to the Baptists for their contribution to the American scene, particularly in relationship to religious liberty.

Autonomous local congregations were the pattern first brought to America by the Pilgrims. This appeared to be very compatible with the temperament of the New World.

The Mayflower bore to Plymouth, in New England, an organized Christian church in general agreement with the Reformed Confession, and a polity combining the principle of the autonomy of the local church with that of the duty of fellowship.[24]

These "dissenters," as they were called when they left the Church of England, moved to Holland and ultimately to the New World because of their convictions about Congregationalism. Their influence on the New World can readily be seen in early American history.

The Holy Scriptures, and especially the scriptures of the New Testament, are the only authoritative rule for constitution of church government; and no other can be imposed on Christians as a condition of membership and communion in the church.[25]

The Cambridge Platform[26]—The dissenters, or Congregationalists, as they identified themselves, wrote *The Cambridge Platform: New England's Handbook of Church Order*. Commenting on this, Alwyn York made a presentation at the 1995 Annual Meeting of the Conservative Congregational Christian Conference in which he asked:

> Should we not be concerned to familiarize ourselves with the conclusions our forefathers reached about theology and church order as they searched the Scriptures on the same basis as we do...? If we claim to be their heirs of faith, should we not at least examine why they thought this way?

The Cambridge document is the definitive statement of church order and discipline produced by the Congregationalists of New England. It was the product of "a transatlantic discussion on the nature of the Church." It was an outgrowth of the Westminster Confession, reflecting what was a "minority view of the Westminster Assembly."

The readers should know that the Cambridge document "did not support an extreme independency," and concerned itself with "the communion of churches with one another, and details of the way this communion is to be exercised."

It restricted membership to "those who could testify to a saving work of grace in their souls, and whose manner of living bore out their profession of faith."

The local churches' structure included "ruling elders," but they defined the "presbytery" as being the elders within a local church and not over a geographical area, as is the custom amongst the Presbyterians.

Unfortunately, Congregationalism became a full-blown denomination under the influence of liberalism and did not follow the example of one of its most outstanding preachers, Jonathan Edwards.

Today, in America

Between 75,000 and 80,000 churches in the United States function as autonomous congregations today, though many of these would hesitate to use the name "Congregational" because of its association with liberalism. These churches form the largest Christian movement in America. We have come almost full circle, yet not quite all the way. The NT began with autonomous local churches. The Reformation opened the way for a return to this primitive pattern though the Reformers did not move all the way into the concept of a regenerate church. It is easier to articulate than to practice.

Today, the largest movement in the United States is the practice of independent or autonomous local churches. It is important, however, for these churches not only to find the NT form of a local church but also to follow the functional pattern for local churches.

What glorious results there would be if these local churches could recover the apostolic mission and pull together for the fulfillment of the Great Commission.

∞ NOTES

[1] Schaff. *History of the Christian Church*. Vol. 3, vol. 8, p. 37.

[2] Paul. *The Church in Search of Its Self*. 74.

[3] Schaff. Op. cit.

[4] Ibid.

[5] Op. cit. 83.

[6] *Ministry of Grace: Studies in Early Church History*. 113,114.

[7] Schaff. Op. cit. Vol. 1, p. 212.

[8] *The Schaff -Herzog Encyclopedia*, Vol. 3, p. 227.

[9] Marsh. *The New Testament Church*. 87.

[10] Lightfoot. *St. Paul's Epistle to the Philippians*. 95.

[11] McGrath. *The Genesis of Doctrine*. 41.

[12] *The Apostolic Fathers*. Edited by Lightfoot. 8.

[13] Ibid. 352.

[14] Ibid. 352.

[15] Gonzalez. *A History of Christian Thought*. 62.

[16] Schaff. *History of the Christian Church*. 226.

[17] Gonzalez. Op. cit. 16.

[18] *The New Schaff-Herzog Encyclopedia*. Vol. 12, p. 464.

[19] Op. cit. 538-540.

[20] Schaff-Herzog, Vol. 1, p. 474.

[21] Schaff. *History of the Christian Church,* Vol. III, p. 235-237.

[22] Bridge and Phypers. *The Water that Divides*. 113, 117.

[23] McBeth. *The Baptist Heritage*. 121, 123.

[24] *Schaff-Herzog Encyclopedia,* Vol. 1, p. 538.

[25] Op. cit.

[26] *The Cambridge Platform*. Edited by Murdy.

CHAPTER TWELVE

THE MISSION OF THE LOCAL CHURCH

Declare his glory among the nations, his marvelous deeds among all peoples. For great is the Lord and most worthy of praise... (Ps. 96:3,4).

GOD IS ON A MISSION

M ission is about God's glory. God's glory is the sum of his attributes as revealed to man. In fact, plans to reveal the glory of God were in process before man was even created.

> *For you know that is was not with perishable things such as silver or gold that you were redeemed from the empty way of life handed down to you from your fore-fathers, but with the precious blood of Christ, a lamb without blemish or defect. He was chosen before the creation of the world, but was revealed in these last times for your sake* (1 Pet. 1:18-20).

There was a cross in the heart of God before he created man and before there was a cross on Calvary's hill.

God is light and God is love. He, by his very nature, *is* mission. He shines. He loves!

For God so **loved** *the world* [only God could love the world in all of its sinfulness] *that He gave his one and only Son* [only God could **so love** the world by the sacrifice on the cross] *that whoever believes in him shall not perish but have eternal life* [only his love could make an eternal difference] (John 3:16).

God sent his Son. Jesus is God's mission!

Mission is laying down one's life for a cause greater than one's self. Jesus loved us and gave himself for us (Gal. 2:20). *"But God demonstrates his own love for us in this: While we were still sinners, Christ died for us"* (Rom. 5:8).

The message of his cross is the heart of mission. This gospel is *"the power of God for the salvation of everyone who believes…"* (Rom. 1:16).

THE PURPOSE AND PLAN OF HIS MISSION

Mission is about the glory of God manifested in the cross. What is this glory? In Jesus' high priestly prayer he prayed, *"Glorify your Son, that your Son may glorify you"* (John 17:1). God's glory for which Christ prayed was revealed in many aspects by the cross. *God's desire* is revealed when Jesus said, *"But I, when I am lifted up from the earth* [crucified], *will draw all men to myself"* (John 12:32).

Mission flows forth from God. His plan is *"to bring all things in heaven and on earth together under one head, even Christ"* (Eph. 1:10). It is for the *"praise of his glorious grace"* (1:6). It is *"according to his good pleasure, which he purposed in Christ"* (1:9). (The more we are under his authority, the more we will be a part of his plan and the more he will be glorified. The issue is submission.)

His infinite holiness was manifest as the righteous judgement of God came on Jesus as our substitute. At the cross we see God's faithfulness to his promise to bring salvation. *His power* is made known when he *"disarmed the powers and authorities... [and] made a public spectacle of them, triumphing over them by the cross"* (Col. 2:15) and *the love of God* finds its fullest disclosure. These and other attributes of God were unveiled to our eyes by Christ's death on the cross.

So the gospel is in fact the declaration of the glory of God. And since *missions* is the work of sharing the gospel of the cross, it is, then, the revelation and declaration of the glory of God. John cites the time when Isaiah saw the Lord's glory (John 12:41) where Isaiah had a vision of the glory filling the earth (Isa. 6:3) which, apparently, was a vision of the gospel going to the whole world. All missionary activity is to make known the glory of God in the whole earth. Missions is a means of glorifying God.

THE CHURCH'S ESSENTIAL FUNCTION

The subtitle of this book is "The Form and Function of the Local Church." The biblical concept requires a description of its purpose and function. Mission is the vital and essential function of the Church. Some would say that it is the *only reason* for the Church's existence, but that isn't exactly true since God's plan for the Church will continue after there is no more need for missions, as we see, *"...to him be glory in the church and in Christ Jesus throughout all generations, for ever and ever"* (Eph. 3:21).

MOTIVATION FOR MISSIONS

The purpose of this chapter is to motivate readers to glorify God by making a greater commitment to the greatest cause on earth—God's mission, the proclamation of his glory. The issue is Jesus Christ, who mandated mission to proclaim the glory of God. He is personally involved, directing and sustaining this mission by his Holy Spirit. It is a part of what we are called to when he called us to be his disciples. It was when Isaiah saw God that he said, *"Here am I, send me"* (Isa. 6:8). Our lack of our vision of God causes our lack of missionary vision.

THE GREAT COMMISSION—OUR MANDATE

When our Lord had risen from the dead he said, *"All authority in heaven and on earth has been given to me. Therefore go and make disciples of all nations..."* (Matt. 28:18,19). His previous command, *"Do not go among the Gentiles"* (Matt. 10:5) was changed. Now it was go to *all nations*. This is the *"mystery of his will"* (Eph. 1:9). That which had been provincial is now global.

Our mandate goes back to Adam's fall; it became more explicit in God's promise to Abraham that he was to be *"heir of the world"* (Rom. 4:13); and even more clear in God's promise that through his seed all the world would be blessed (Gen. 12:3).

Someone has said this promise is the "grandest of all missionary texts," and some have called it "the spinal cord of missions." As Israel had a mandate to possess the Land, the Christian community has a mandate to possess the world. As the Lord said to Israel, *"I will give you every place where you set your foot"* (Josh. 1:3), so Isaiah foresaw the possession of the mountains (nations) in our time. Paul joins the passages together, *"How beautiful on the mountains are the feet of those who bring good news..."* (Isa. 52:7; Rom. 10:15).

Israel had a mandate to be a light to the nations, but Israel defined that role in military and political terms. So

Israel expected a political and military leader but instead was sent a spiritual Savior. They looked for a king and a general, and they got a farmer sowing seeds (Matt. 13). Swords were to be replaced with seeds.

We read in Isaiah 49:6, *"I will also make a light for the Gentiles, that you may bring my salvation to the ends of the earth."* Paul tells us that this promise is fulfilled in and through Israel's greater son, Jesus Christ (Acts 13:47).

THE SPHERE OF MISSIONS

"The field is the world…" (Matt. 13:38). The provincial must give way to the global. It is his harvest field and the harvest is his. The word "world" must have impacted Jesus' Jewish audience as radical and revolutionary.

The future has arrived! *"Indeed, all the prophets from Samuel on, as many as have spoken, have foretold these days"* (Acts 3:24). It is not sometime or somewhere, but it is here and now. *"Now is the day of salvation"* (2 Cor. 6:2).

JESUS IS THE MISSION DIRECTOR.

He directs through the ministry of the Holy Spirit, as we see throughout the book of Acts. First, he says, "wait" (1:4). Then he announces the new program which crosses all barriers—racial, generational, and social, as well as gender. *"I will pour out my Spirit on all people… sons and daughters… young and old… men and women…"* (2:17,18). He rules and overrules, even making *"the wrath of men to praise him"* (Ps. 76:10 KJV), in such cases as Paul's imprisonment in Rome. He takes a leader out of a revival and gives him specific instructions on how to reach one individual (8:26-29). He calls into apostle-ship the most unlikely man—Saul (9:6,15,16). He calls

161

the church at Antioch, *not* Jerusalem, to send forth the first missionaries (13:2-4). He oversaw and guided another messenger to cross the barriers of bigotry and race to reach a Gentile (10:9-38). He confirmed the message of his messengers (10:45,46; 13:8-11; 14:3). To his churches he revealed his program to bring in the Gentiles and save them through grace (15:7-9). He stopped them from preaching in Asia (16:6) and led them in a different direction than they had planned.

The story goes on and on until this very day. He is the primary mission director.

JESUS' CALL TO MISSION

He first calls us to himself. He *"called to him those he wanted.... He appointed twelve... that they might be with him... that he might send them..."* (Mark 3:13,14). He "rubs off" on those close to him. His vision must become the vision of his followers. His cross was in view as were their crosses. There was no doubt as to the cost of being a disciple. Jesus must become everything, and all else must fade into relative insignificance. The disciples must study their Lord. *"A student is not above his teacher, nor a servant above his master. It is enough for the student to be like his teacher..."* (Matt. 10:24,25).

The Lord's call came to the first disciples as he taught and performed miracles in their midst. His call now comes to us from the cross!

> *Therefore, I urge you, brothers, in view of God's mercy, to offer your bodies as living sacrifices, holy and pleasing to God—which is your spiritual worship...* (Rom. 12:1).

This presentation precedes transformation. It also precedes what Paul writes about gifts and ministries in the same chapter. Our availability is what he asks. His ability is what he gives.

Our service, on the mission field or wherever we are, is our worship of our Lord. Missionary activity is first an act of worship (Rom. 15:16-18). Our service is centered in the Lord and not simply in our feelings for the needy. The glory of God is primary. "Man's chief end is to glorify God and enjoy him forever," reads the Westminster Confession. In today's time when "worship" is the focus of attention, we need to re-discover this dimension of worship.

When the Lord calls us, he calls us to be with him. If he calls us to the mission field, it is because he is already there preparing hearts to receive his messengers.

When he calls us, it is to go with him and not to go alone. It is in connection with the Great Commission that he says, *"And surely I will be with you always, to the very end of the age"* (Matt. 28:20). He doesn't come to observe but to work. We are his *"fellow-workers"* (1 Cor. 3:9). He is so present in the apostles' preaching that their preaching is said to be his preaching (Eph. 2:17). They *"preached the gospel to you by the Holy Spirit sent from heaven"* (1 Pet. 1:12) And it is in their preaching that his other sheep hear his voice (John 10:16).

We must also remember that when we see the harvest, we are not told to choose a field and go to it, but we are told to pray that the Lord of the harvest would send forth his reapers according to his will.

THE VISION OF THE MISSION FIELD

What we see is a hopeless condition and problems that

are too great for us to solve. Man is lost! He is a "fallen man." He is dead in trespasses and sins. History's description of man's lostness fills many books. What man has done to his fellow man has exposed his lost condition. G. K. Chesterton has said that the only doctrine in Scripture that can be empirically proven is the depravity of man. And it is in view of man's condition that we read, *"...the Son of Man came to seek and save what was lost"* (Luke 19:10). If one would protest that he is not lost, that one must acknowledge that the Son of Man did not come for him. It is because of the condition of man that Paul writes, *"There is no one righteous, not even one... no one who seeks God.... There is no one who does good..."* (Rom. 3:10-12).

Such a condition requires the supernatural, and I am not just talking about physical miracles but I am talking about the drawing power of God: *"...no one can come to me unless the Father has enabled him"* (John 6:65). The dead must hear the resurrecting voice of the Son of God in order to live (John 5:25). Or, in the words of my late friend, Pastor Roy Johnson, who when speaking of preaching said, "We preach; but then, the real preacher is the Holy Spirit."

THE UNIQUENESS OF JESUS CHRIST

"Salvation is found in no one else, for there is no other name under heaven given to men by which we must be saved" (Acts 4:12). He is the only Savior. He is the only way. In our pluralistic society this is being challenged today as never before.

Consider Jesus' words: *"...I am the gate for the sheep... whoever enters through me will be saved"* (John. 10:7,9). He contrasted himself with others and described them as thieves and robbers.

In addition, consider these things about Jesus that are not true of anyone else:

- *he is the only one about whom a book was written before he was born;*
- *he is the only one who provides salvation through his own death;*
- *he is the only one who promises forgiveness and eternal life by trusting in him;*
- *he is he only one who based the credibility of his promise on the fact of his resurrection* (Rom. 1:4).

We believe in him and not just in a formula or a set of propositions. He then takes us by the hand and leads us into the fullness of life.

Now consider the challenges as presented by Ravi Zacharias:

Jesus... stated that God is the Author of life and that meaning in life lies in coming to Him. This assertion would be categorically denied by Buddhism, which is a non-theistic if not atheistic religion.... Jesus revealed himself as the Son of God who led the way to the Father. Islam considers that claim to be blasphemous. How can God have a Son? ...Jesus claimed that we can personally know God and the absolute nature of His truth. Agnostics deny that possibility.[1]

Jesus is the incomparable Savior and the only hope of lost mankind. His exclusivity is foundational to missions.

THE MISSIONARY MESSAGE

No message other than the gospel of our Lord Jesus Christ even pretends to reveal God, bring man to God, and assure him forgiveness and eternal life. It alone is the power of God unto salvation.

More attention needs to be given to the message instead of having our main focus be centered on methods. One of the great burdens of the New Testament was to preserve the message of the gospel. In Paul's writings alone we find the word "gospel" over seventy times.

What you heard from me, keep as the pattern of sound teaching, with faith and love in Christ Jesus. Guard the good deposit... with the help of the Holy Spirit who lives in us (2 Tim. 1:13,14).

Without question, the most succinct statement of the gospel is found in Paul's first letter to the Corinthians:

Now brothers, I want to remind you of the gospel I preached to you, which you received and on which you have taken your stand. By this gospel you are saved, if you hold firmly to the word I preached to you.... For what I received I passed on to you as of first importance that Christ died for our sins according to the Scriptures, that he was buried, that he was raised the third day according to the Scriptures (15:1-4).

This salvation by God's grace manifest in the Christ-event separates the gospel from all other messages of the religions of the world. They proclaim salvation by works, self-discovery, political liberation, metaphysics, etc. Even the Pope himself failed the world when he proclaimed salvation by works when he said:

Those who have chosen the way of the Gospel Beatitudes and live as he, 'poor in spirit,' detached from material goods, in order to raise up the lowly of the earth from the dust of their humiliation, will enter the kingdom of God.[2]

CROSSING THE BARRIERS

There are spiritual, social, economic, cultural, and language barriers, to name a few, not the least of which is this fact:

The god of this age has blinded the minds of unbelievers, so that they cannot see the light of the gospel of the glory of Christ... (2 Cor. 4:4).

Communication is one of our greatest problems. The problem, however, is first of all in us, for what we are communicating is a fire and not a picture of the fire. We must be "on fire" to ignite anyone else.

Don Smith, in his lectures, "What the Bible Really Says About Missions," tells the story of a certain godly Scotsman.

Every morning before he left his home to work in a grimy factory of Glasgow, he gave time—a half an hour, one hour—to be quiet before God, a communion with him. A neighbor spoke of him with awe, "Every morning he comes out of that little house glowing. What he is I want to become." The Scotsman knew that real living began with real communion, foundational communication.

We are transmitting life, not just information.

John Piper writes:

Missionaries will never call out, "Let the Nations be glad!" who cannot say from the heart, "I will rejoice in the Lord.... I will be glad, I rejoice in the Lord.... I will be glad and exult in thee."[3]

If missions is a form of worship, it must begin with the primacy of worship. Dave Hall writes:

In God's divine economy, it is 'worshiper first, mom second; worshiper first, husband second; worshiper first, missionary second.'[4]

If the church is to be relevant and credible, it is imperative for Christians to express a sense of social justice and to speak out on behalf of the weak and oppressed. It must not be seen as simply the supporter of the status quo.

Charles Spurgeon confronted the hyper-Calvinists of his day saying that the fundamental need for preachers is to know more comm=union with Christ himself.[5] That great soul-winner, Charles Spurgeon, was convinced the lack of soul-winning passion arose from a lack of closeness to Christ.

MISSIONS IS SERVING GOD.

Our service is to God. It is not serving results. It is God *"who makes things grow"* (1 Cor. 3:7).

Here are two examples. The first is Adoniram Judson, America's first foreign missionary, who served eight years before there were ten converts. During that time Judson and his wife suffered the loss of two children, one still-born and the other by a tropical fever. Second, Elizabeth Elliott tells of how she learned she was serving the Lord and not results when she suffered the loss of her husband when he was martyred by the Auca Indians, the loss of the only Indian (by death) who could assist with her translation of the Scriptures, and then finally the loss of the manuscript with which she was working. It was then that it came forcibly home to her that she was serving the One who said:

Do not be afraid, I am the First and the Last. I am the Living One; I was dead, and behold I am alive for ever and ever! And I hold the keys of death and Hades (Rev. 1:17,18).

When she realized whom she was serving, she found strength to go on and do a great work.

THE LOCAL CHURCH AND MISSIONS

Our missionary activity arises from our very nature in Christ as light. He who said, *"I am the light of the world"* (John 8:12) also said to his disciples, *"You are the light of the world"* (Matt. 5:14). Paul, referring to Isaiah's prophecy that Israel would be a "light to the Gentiles," says, *"the Lord has commanded us: 'I have made you a light for the Gentiles...'"* (Acts 13:47).

Local churches are divine lighthouses and missionary outposts. That is the pattern in the book of Acts:

While they [the local church at Antioch] *were worshiping the Lord and fasting, the Holy Spirit said, "Set apart for me Barnabas and Saul for the work to which I have called them." So after they had fasted and prayed, they placed their hands on them and sent them off* (Acts 13:2,3).

Amazingly, it was from Antioch and not Jerusalem, and the finest of their leaders were sent. It was a local church which sent them, and it was to that same church that they returned and reported of their work (Acts 14:27). And it was the church at Antioch that stood by them when certain men sought to undermine their missionary work (Acts 15:2). From this example we see that people sent by a local church are accountable to that church and local churches are accountable to their missionaries.

The practice of missions begins with the local church. This is where the vision is taught, where people are equipped for *"works of service"* (Eph. 4:12), where the potential missionary's call is recognized, and where they are encouraged. It is where one is ordained, and requirements for ordination are visible to a local church and are not at a national level (1 Tim. 3).

The local church, realizing that it is the primary cog in the missionary machinery, teaches missions at every level from the youngest Sunday School class on up, promotes missions, and supports missions with their finances, prayer, letters and on-going contacts.

The Great Commission is not just to us as individuals but is a commission to and of the local church. Johannes Blauw said, "No longer is the 'point of departure'... the Temple but rather the congregation."[6]

When a local church grasps its responsibility to both the Lord and its constituents, then it will have taken a major step forward into fulfilling its God-given task. This is not where missions ends, but where it begins.

However, there are numerous tasks which cannot be done by a single church. Cooperation and collaboration are essential. The task is like war time—it requires full mobilization of personnel and resources.

Church boards need to think of themselves as mission boards and, with the pastor, oversee the mission of their church. They will never fulfill their potential while they leave this task to someone else or to another organization.

It was when A. J. Gordon grasped the reality of Christ in the midst of his church in Boston that he reorganized his church from top to bottom. The end result was that his church became one of the foremost missionary churches in the world.

Things reproduce after their own kind. Missions from the local churches in turn produce other local churches. Churches plant churches. The churches they plant in turn become missionary societies in themselves. These are indigenous, self-governing, self-supporting, and self-propagating. They need not wait for anyone to get on with the task. God calls churches to mission just as he calls individuals to specific roles in his harvest field.

LEADERSHIP FOR MISSIONS

The person normally used of God to lead a local church into effective missions is the pastor. As noted earlier, a pastor of a church is to be the leader of the leaders. This places the responsibility on him to lead in missions.

Missions is not done by accident but by intention. Churches which respond to the Lord's call to missions need to develop a mission statement. Just as Jesus began his public ministry with a mission statement, *"He has sent me... to proclaim the year of the Lord's favor"* (Luke 4:18,19), so a church needs to prayerfully and studiously write its own mission statement.

Missions must be studied, both in Scripture and in a world of need. Boundless resources are available. Missionaries themselves are a primary source, and missionaries need to realize that, when they visit a church, their purpose is both to impart vision and to educate a congregation for missions.

Missions are the life of the Church, both locally and in the field. This "life" is experienced in sharing the gospel with others. It is the heartbeat of God. When we are one with him, we are one with his redemptive purpose. When we are filled with the Holy Spirit, we are "in step with the Spirit." Henry Martyn said, "The Spirit of Christ is the spirit of missions, and the nearer we get to him the more intensely missionary minded we become."

WHERE MISSIONS BEGIN

The vision and work of missions doesn't begin with an ocean voyage or an airplane ride. It begins in the local church and in our neighborhoods. The unsaved world is next door. People who can't begin here are unlikely to begin anywhere. We live in a time when God, in his providence, has literally brought the foreign field to our very doorstep. If we don't have any burden for the Latins around us, the Asian immigrants next door, the Black community in our midst, or any of the other people groups surrounding us, let us not feel our mission can miraculously begin with a trip to South America, Asia, Africa, or wherever else we might go.

THE COST OF MISSIONS

Our planning and budget must reflect our sense of vision and our call to be employed in the Lord's harvest.

As reported in a *Barna Report,*[7] churches in the United States give an average of 16 percent of their budget to missions, a figure which seems very high compared to the churches with which I am familiar. Our missionary giving is more like a thermostat than a thermometer. Ralph Johnson once said, "A thermometer merely reflects the temperature in a room, whereas a thermostat determines it."

The cost of missions is identical today to the cost in the early Church. It costs the lives of those yielding to the missionary vision. In fact, that is precisely what Jesus said about following him.

MONEY AND MISSIONS

Where people have a vision for missions, they will not be satisfied with the amount of money raised for the missionary cause. Where there is a true missionary vision the costs will not be too high, but where there is a lack of vision the financial costs will always to be too much.

When one brings up the subject of missions, people immediately think of money. The dollar costs intimidate many. Financial concerns hinder many churches from responding, and yet these costs continue to rise.

> Today's support levels range between $25,000 and $80,000 a year. It is startling to think of future missionaries raising a $100,000 a year for support.... There are presently 61 countries around the world where the cost of living is higher than downtown New York City.[8]

While thinking of the financial costs, remember how much more you pay for a new car or home these days. Also remember that God measures our giving by what we have left after we give. (The Christian Booksellers Association recently reported that Christians are spending an average of five billion dollars a year on books, which tells us something of our potential.)

To put this into a different perspective, consider the story of the Cambridge Seven:

> Seven young aristocratic athletes from Cambridge stunned England in the latter part of the last [nineteenth] century when they renounced fame and fortune to serve Christ as missionaries with the China Inland Mission. Before leaving for the mission field they

toured the British Isles, speaking at colleges and universities. These, 'the Cambridge Seven,' catapulted the China Inland Mission to the attention of the world. When they arrived in China in 1885 CIM had 163 missionaries and by 1900 there were 800.[9]

There is a river of blood that has flowed throughout Church history, and it is the blood of those who have given their lives to share the gospel with others.

If the Church is to be the Church, it must be a missionary Church. Churches built on the foundation of the apostles must incorporate both the apostles' *message* and *mission*. That is what it means to be an apostolic church. Dietrich Bonhoeffer said:

> The Church is not a religious community of worshipers of Christ, but it is Christ himself who has taken form among men.[10]

We are the body of Christ, the incarnation, the incorporation of the great Missionary, Jesus Christ. We cannot be his disciples without taking up our cross and following him wherever he leads.

Wallace Alston, Jr., recorded some of Karl Barth's thoughts.[11] Barth commented that there is a "yawning gap" in the Reformed doctrine of the Church created by the absence of any sense of the Church's mission in and to the world. Barth asked, "Why does the church exist? ...Surely God did not create the church only to be the mother of the faithful." Barth calls this the "holy egoism" of the Church.

Consider also Craig Van Gelder's observation that:

> Local congregations are the primary and most assessable structure of the organizational development of the visible church.[12]

It is the ATV (all-terrain-vehicle) for missions. It is viable everywhere and anywhere. It is a "sailing ship," and not a large rowing ship. All it needs is the "wind" of God. It needn't be large but if it happens to be, that is not a problem either.

This is where the "rubber touches the road" because this is where the primary support, both spiritually and financially, is raised for missions. This reality and responsibility cannot be lifted from local churches and placed upon missionary societies and parachurch groups or any hierarchal structure, though these may provide a valuable servant role. If this burden is shifted from the local church to a supervisory body, it will be at the cost of lack of the development of the local churches. Today, there is a movement to networking that (and this, to a great degree) makes the hierarchal administration superfluous.

May God help all of us visualize the potential of the vast number of independent/local churches networking together to fulfill our Lord's commission.

A COMPARISON OF SUPPORT— LARGE AND SMALL

An indication of the ability of local churches to do missionary work can be seen when comparing the Assemblies of God (AOG), a very large denomination known for its missionary success, with the much smaller Fellowship of Christian Assemblies (FCA), an association of autonomous churches. In a recent comparison, the latter is made up of 113 churches which support 233 active missionaries functioning in sixty-three fields. (This did not include those working with parachurches, such YWAM.) On the other hand, the large organization is made up of 12,055 US churches supporting 1,814 active missionaries functioning in 181 fields.

Here is the math: The FCA has 2.6 active missionaries per church and the AOG has one active missionary for every 6.6 churches. (The AOG statistics are from the *Division of Foreign Missions—2000 Annual Stats,* Dec. 31, 1999, and the FCA stats are from the *Directory & Resource Guide of the FCA for Year 2000.* The AOG stats include mission fields where there is no American representative, which is not reported that way in the FCA directory.)

I know enough about statistics to know this is probably not a completely accurate picture, but it is enough to demonstrate that local churches can effectively do missionary work.

POTENTIAL

Then, of course, none of us even begins to do what we could do.

Elizabeth Elliott quotes her husband's forceful words,

We cuddle around the Lord's table as though it were the last coal of God's altar, and warm our hands, thinking that will appease the wrath of the indignant Christ when He charges us with unmet, unchallenged, untaught generations of the heathen now doing their Christmas shopping.... Believers who know one-tenth as much as we do are doing one hundred times more for God, with His blessing and our criticism.[13]

So let us not suppose we have even begun to realize our potential. Let us hear God's call to awake from our sleep and experience his great promise:

Wake up, O sleeper,
Rise from the dead,
And Christ will shine on you.

(Eph. 5:14)

A passage in Isaiah also emphasizes the missionary successes of the responsive ones:

...the Lord rises upon you and his glory appears over you. Nations will come to your light, and kings to the brightness of your dawn (Isa. 60:2,3).

May each of us as individuals and as local churches awake and arise to the fulfillment of this great missionary promise of our Lord.

May our Lord be glorified!

∽ NOTES

[1] Zacharias. *Jesus Among Other Gods.* 5.

[2] As reported in *L'Osservatore Romano.* Dec. 13, 2000.

[3] Piper. *Let the Nations be Glad.* 11.

[4] *The Evangelical Missions Quarterly.* 2000.

[5] Murray. *Spurgeon Vs. Hyper-Calvinism.* 94.

[6] Blauw. *The Missionary Nature of the Church.* 91.

[7] *Your Church.* April-June 1999.

[8] Seger, Paul. *The Vision.* January/February 1999, p. 13.

[9] Morgan. *On This Day.* Dec. 9.

[10] Bonhoeffer. *A Discussion of Christian Fellowship.*

[11] Alston. *Guides to the Reformed Tradition.*

[12] Van Gelder. *The Essence of the Church—a Community Created by the Spirit.* 166.

[13] Elliott. *Shadow of the Almighty.* 138.

SELECTED BIBLIOGRAPHY

Alston, Wallace M., Jr. *The Church—Guides to the Reformed Tradition*. Richmond, Va.: John Knox Press, 1934.

The Analytical Greek Lexicon. Grand Rapids, Mich.: Zondervan Publishing House, 1970.

And He Gave Pastors: Pastoral Theology in Action. Edited by Thomas F. Zimmerman. Springfield, Mo.: Gospel Publishing House, 1979.

Anderson, Robert C. *The Effective Pastor: A Practical Guide to the Ministry*. Chicago, Ill.: Moody Press, 1985.

The Apostolic Fathers. Edited by Jack N. Sparks. New York: Thomas Nelson, Inc. Publishers.

The Apostolic Fathers: Clement, Ignatius, and Polycarp. Second edition, 2 parts in 5 vols. Edited by J. B. Lightfoot. Peabody, Mass.: Hendrickson Publishers.

Armerding, Hudson T. *Leadership*. Wheaton, Ill.: Tyndale House Publishers, Inc., 1978.

Arrington, French L. *Divine Order in the Church: A study of 1 Corinthians*. Grand Rapids, Mich.: Baker Book House, 1978 & 1981.

Bakke, Ray. *A Theology As Big As the City*. Downers Grove, Ill.: Inter-Varsity Press, 1997.

Balswick, Judith & Boni Piper. *Life Ties: Cultivating Relationships That Make Life Worth Living*. Downers Grove, Ill.: Inter-Varsity Press. 1995.

Banks, Robert. *Paul's Idea of Community: The Early House Churches in Their Historical Setting*. Grand Rapids, Mich.: Wm. B. Eerdmans Publishing Company, 1980.

Barna, George. *Leaders on Leadership: Wisdom, Advice and Encouragement on the Art of Leading God's People*. Ventura, Calif.: Regal Books/Gospel Light, 1997.

Bauer, Arndt, and Gingrich. *The Greek English Lexicon of the New Testament*. Chicago, Ill.: University of Chicago Press.

Baughen, Michael. *The Moses Principle: Leadership and the Venture of Faith*. Wheaton, Ill.: Harold Shaw Publishers, 1978.

Beals, Paul A. *A People for His Name: A Church-Based Missions Strategy*. Pasadena, Calif.: William Carey Library.

Bedsole, Adolph. *The Pastor in Profile*. Grand Rapids, Mich.: Baker Book House, 1958.

Berkhof, Hendrikus. *Christian Faith: An Introduction to the Study of the Faith*. Grand Rapids, Mich.: Wm. B. Eerdmans Publishing Company, 1979.

Bigg, Rev. Charles. *A Critical and Exegetical Commentary on the Epistles of St. Peter and St. Jude*. Edinburgh: T. & T. Clark.

Bigg. *The New International Critical Commentary, St. Peter and St. Jude*. Edinburgh: T. & T. Clark.

Blackwood, Andrew Watterson. *Pastoral Leadership*. New York: Abingdon-Cokesbury Press, 1959.

Blauw, Johannes. *The Missionary Nature of the Church*. Grand Rapids, Mich.: Wm. B. Eerdmans Publishing Company.

Bonhoeffer, Dietrich. *Life Together: A Discussion of Christian Fellowship*. Translated with an introduction by John W. Doberstein. San Francisco, Calif.: Harper & Row, Publishers, 1954.

Booth, Gordon T. *Evangelical & Congregational*. The Principles of the Congregational Independents with the Savoy Declaration of Faith and Order. 9th Edition. Ware, England: Evangelical Fellowship of Evangelical Churches, 1981.

Brethren, High Leigh Conference of. *A New Testament Church in 1955*. Great Britain, Stanley L. Hunt Ltd.

Bridge, Donald and David Phypers. *The Water that Divides*. Downers Grove, Ill.: Inter-Varsity Press.

Bultmann, Rudolf. *Primitive Christianity in its Contemporay Setting*. Translated by Rev. R. H. Fuller. New York: Living Age Books: published by Meridian Books.

Bush, Laura Duvall. *Breaking Down the Walls: 9 Studies from Ephesians on Relationships in Christ*. Wheaton, Ill.: Victor Books, a division of Scripture Press Publications, Inc., 1989.

Cairns, Earle E. *Christianity Through the Centuries: A History of the Christian Church*. Third edition. Grand Rapids, Mich.: Zondervan Publishing House.

Callahan, Kennon L. *Effective Church Leadership: Building on the Twelve Keys*. San Francisco, Calif.: Harper & Row, Publishers, 1990.

Calvin, John. *Commentaries on the Epistles of Paul: 1 & II Timothy and Titus*. Translated from the original Latin by Rev. William Pringle. Grand Rapids, Mich.: Baker Book House.

The Cambridge Platform. Edited by Peter Murdy. Millers Falls, Mass.: First Congregational Church, 1998.

Carey Conference. *The Ideal Church: Papers Read at the Carey Conference in July, 1971*. Foxton, England: Carey Publications Ltd., 1972.

Carroll, B. H. *Ecclesia (The Church)*. Little Rock, Ark.: The Challenge Press.

Clower, Joseph B., Jr. *The Church in the Thought of Jesus*. Richmond, Va.: John Knox Press, 1959.

Clowney, Edmund P. *The Church: Contours of Christian Theology*. Downers Grove, Ill.: Inter-Varsity Press, 1995.

Coates, C.A. *The House of God*. Kingston-On-Thames, England: Stow Hill Bible and Tract Depot.

Colson, Charles, with Ellen Santtilli Vaughn. *The Body: Being*

Light in Darkness. Dallas, Tex.: Word Publishing, 1992-1997.

Confessing Christ as Lord: The Urbana 81 Compendium. Edited by John W. Alexander. Downers Grove, Ill.: Inter-Varsity Press, 1982.

Congregations: Their Power to Form and Transform. Edited by C. Ellis Nelson. Atlanta, Ga.: John Knox Press, 1988.

Conybeare, Rev. W. J. and Rev. J. S. Howson. *The Life and Epistles of St. Paul.* Grand Rapids, Mich.: Wm. B. Eerdmans Publishing Company, 1966.

Creeds of the Churches. Third edition. Edited by John H. Leith. Atlanta, Ga.: John Knox Press, 1973.

Criswell, W. A. *Criswell's Guidebook for Pastors.* Nashville, Tenn.: Broadman Press, 1980.

Cullmann, Oscar. *Early Christian Worship.* Translated by A. Stewart Todd and James B. Torrance. London: SCM Press.

Cutts, Rev. Edward L. *Turning Points of General Church History.* New York: E. & J. B. Young & Co., 1893.

Dale, R. W. *A Manual of Congregational Principles.* London: Hodder and Stoughton, 1884.

Dale. *The Jewish Temple and the Christian Church: A Series of Discourses on the Epistle to the Hebrews.* Eleventh Edition. London: Hodder and Stoughton, 1902.

Davies, W. D. *A Normative Pattern of Church Life in the New Testament: Fact or Fancy?* London: James Clarke & Co. Ltd., Publishers.

DeVille, Jard. *Pastor's Handbook on Interpersonal Relationships: Keys to Successful Leadership.* Grand Rapids, Mich.: Baker Book House, 1986.

Draper, James T., Jr. *Titus: Patterns for Church Living.* Wheaton, Ill.: Tyndale House Publishers, Inc., 1978.

Edersheim, Alfred. *The Temple—Its Ministry and Services.* Grand Rapids, Mich.: Wm. B. Eerdmans Publishing Company.

Elliott, Elizabeth. *Shadow of the Almighty*. New York: Harper & Brothers.

Elliott. *Through Gates of Splendor*. New York: Harper & Brothers, 1957.

Engelsma, Rev. David J. *The Church Today and The Reformation Church: A Comparison*. South Holland, Ill.: The Evangelism Committee, South Holland Protestant Reformed Church, 1972.

Erdman, Charles R. *The Work of the Pastor*. Philadelphia, Pa.: The Westminster Press, 1928.

Erickson, Millard J. *Christian Theology*. Unabridged, one-volume edition. Grand Rapids, Mich.: Baker Book House, 1983, 1984, 1985.

Eusebius Pamphilus. *Eusebius' Ecclesiastical History*. Translated from the original with an introduction by Christian Frederick Cruse and an historical view of The Council of Nice by Isaac Boyle. Grand Rapids, Mich.: Baker Book House, 1962.

Farrar, Frederick. *The History of Interpretation*. New York: E. P. Dutton and Co., 1885.

Fee, Gordon D. *The First Epistle to the Corinthians*. Grand Rapids, Mich.: Wm. B. Eerdmans Publishing Company.

Fee. *New International Biblical Commentary: I & II Timothy, Titus*. Edited by Ward Gasque. Peabody, Mass.: Hendrickson Publishers.

Ford, Leighton. *Transforming Leadership: Jesus' Way of Creating Vision, Shaping Values & Empowering Change*. Downers Grove, Ill.: Inter-Varsity Press, 1991.

Fredrikson, Roger L. *The Church That Refused to Die: A Powerful Story of Reconciliation and Renewal*. Wheaton, Ill.: Victor Books, Scripture Press Publications, 1991.

Geisler, Norman and Ralph McKenzie. *Roman Catholics and Evangelicals*. Grand Rapids, Mich.: Baker Book House.

Giles, Kevin. *What On Earth Is the Church?: An Exploration In New Testament Theology*. Downers Grove, Ill.: Inter-Varsity

Press, 1995.

Glover, Robert Hall, M.D. *The Bible Basis of Missions*. Los Angeles, Calif.: Bible House of Los Angeles, 1946.

Gonzalez, Justo L. *A History of Christian Thought*. Vols. I, II & III. Nashville, Tenn.: Abingdon Press.

Greanleaf, Robert K. *Servant Leadership*. Mahwah, N.J.: Paulist Press, 1977.

Green, Michael. *Evangelism in the Early Church*. Glasgow: HarperCollins Manufacturing, 1970.

Grenz, Stanley J. *Revisioning Evangelical Theology: A Fresh Agenda for the 21st Century*. Downers Grove, Ill.: Inter-Varsity Press, 1993.

Griffiths, Michael. *Timothy and Titus*. Grand Rapids, Mich.: Baker Book House.

Guinness, Os. *The Call: Finding and Fulfilling the Central Purpose of your Life*. Nashville, Tenn.: Word Publishing, 1998.

Hall, Eddy and Gary Morsch. *The Lay Ministry Revolution: How You Can Join*. Grand Rapids, Mich.: Baker Books, 1995.

Halverson, Richard. *The Living Body: The Church Christ Is Building*. Gresham,Ore.: Vision House.

Hardesty, Nancy A. *Inclusive Language in the Church*. Atlanta, Ga.: John Knox Press, 1946, 1952 & 1971.

Hay, Alexander Rattray. *The New Testament Order for Church and Missionary*. Third edition by the New Testament Missionary Union. Printed in the Netherlands: H.H. Block.

Hayford, Jack. *Pastors of Promise: Pointing to Character and Hope As the Keys to Fruitful Shepherding*. Ventura, Calif.: Regal Books, a Division of Gospel Light, 1997.

Heckman, Warren L. *History of the Fellowship of Christian Assemblies*. Madison, Wis.: Fellowship Press, 1994.

Hendricksen, William. *New Testament Commentary*. Grand Rapids, Mich.: Baker Book House.

Here We Stand: A Call From Confessing Evangelicals. Edited by

James Montgomery Boice and Benjamin E. Sasse. Grand Rapids, Mich.: Baker Books, 1996.

History of the Christian Church. Edited by Phillip Schaff. 3 vols. New York: Funk and Wagnalls, 1883.

Jacobsen, Wayne. *The Naked Church*. Eugene, Ore.: Harvest House Publishers, 1987.

Jarrel, W. A. *Baptist Church Perpetuity or the Continuous Existence of Baptist Churches from the Apostolic to the Present Day Demonstrated by the Bible and by History*. Third edition. Fulerton, Ky.: National Baptist Publishing House, 1904.

Johnson, Harold E. *Mentoring for Exceptional Performance*. Glendale, Calif.: Griffin Publishing, 1997.

Johnson, Luke Timothy. *Knox Preaching Guides: 1 Timothy, II Timothy and Titus*. Edited by John H. Hayes. Atlanta, Ga.: John Knox Press.

Jones, Ilion T. *A Historical Approach to Evangelical Worship*. New York: Abingdon Press, 1954.

Jones, Laurie Beth. *Jesus C E O: Using Ancient Wisdom for Visionary Leadership*. New York: Hyperion, 1995.

Jones, Philip L. *A Restatement of Baptist Principles*. Philadelphia, Pa.: The Griffith & Rowland Press, 1909.

Kerr, William F., D.D. *Conservative Baptist Distinctives*. Portland, Ore.: Western Conservative Baptist Seminary, 1965, 1975.

King, David S. *No Church Is An Island*. New York: The Pilgrim Press, 1980.

Kline, Meredith G. *By Oath Consigned*. Grand Rapids, Mich.: Wm. B. Eerdmans Publishing Company, 1968.

Kline. *The Structure of Biblical Authority*. Grand Rapids, Mich.: Wm. B. Eerdmans Publishing Company, 1972.

Kohl, Manfred Waldemar. *Congregationalism in America*. Oak Creek, Wis.: The Congregational Press, 1977.

Kraft, Charles H. *Christianity in Culture: A study in Dynamic Biblical Theologizing in Cross-Cultural Perspective*. Maryknoll, N.Y.: Orbis Books, 1979.

Kroll, Woodrow. *The Vanishing Ministry.* Grand Rapids, Mich.: Kregel Publications, 1991.

Kuen, Alfred F. *I Will Build My Church.* Translated by Ruby Lindblad. Chicago, Ill.: Moody Press, 1971.

Kung, Hans. *Structures of the Church.* New York: Thomas Nelson & Sons, 1964.

Lenski, R. C. H. *The Interpretation of St. Paul's First and Second Epistles to the Corinthians.* Minneapolis, Minn.: Augsburg Publishing House.

Lenski. *The Interpretation of St. Paul's Epistles to the Galatians, to the Ephesians, and to the Philippians.* Minneapolis, Minn.: Augsburg Publishing House.

LePeau, Andrew T. *Paths of Leadership.* Downers Grove, Ill.: Inter-Varsity Press, 1983.

Lewis, C. S. *God in the Dock.* Grand Rapids, Mich.: Wm. B. Eerdmans Publishing Company, 1970.

Lightfoot, J. B. *St. Paul's Epistle to the Philippians.* Grand Rapids, Mich.: Zondervan.

Lloyd-Jones, D. Martyn. *I Am Not Ashamed: Advice to Timothy.* Grand Rapids, Mich.: Baker Book House, 1986.

Lock, Rev. Walter. *A Critical and Exegetical Commentary on the Pastoral Epistles: I & II Timothy and Titus.* Edinburgh: T. & T. Clark.

Lock. *The International Critical Commentary.* Edinburgh: T. & T. Clark.

London, H. B., Jr. and Neil B. Wiseman. *Pastor At Risk.* Wheaton, Ill.: Victor Books/Scripture Press Publications Inc., 1993.

Lueker, Erwin L. *Lutheran Cyclopedia.* St. Louis, Mo.: Concordia Publishing House.

Luther, Martin. *Works of Martin Luther.* The Philadelphia Edition. Grand Rapids, Mich.: Baker Book House, Reprinted 1982.

Macarthur, John, Jr. *The Ultimate Priority On Worship*. Chicago, Ill.: Moody Press.

Marsh, Rev. W. H. H. *The New Testament Church*. Philadelphia, Pa.: American Baptist Publication Society, 1898.

Marshall, I. Howard. *The IVP New Testament Commentary Series: I Peter*. Grant R. Osborne, series editor; D. Stuart Briscoe and Haddon Robinson, consulting editors. Downers Grove, Ill.: Inter-Varsity Press.

Marshall, Paul. *Their Blood Cries Out*. Dallas, Tex.: Word Publishing.

Mauro, Philip. *The Church, The Churches and the Kingdom*. Washington, D.C.: The Perry Studio, 1936.

McBeth, H. Leon. *The Baptist Heritage*. Nashville, Tenn.: Broadman, 1987.

McBirnie, William Steuart. *The Search for the Early Church New Testament Principles for Today's Church*. Wheaton, Ill.: Tyndale House Publishers, Inc., 1978.

McGrath, Alistair E. *The Genesis of Doctrine*. Grand Rapids, Mich.: Wm. B. Eerdmans Publishing Company, 1990.

Merrill, Rev. Daryl R. *God's Order for the Local Church: A Study of New Testament Principles for Local Church Government*. A Doctoral Dissertation presented to Columbia Pacific University by the author.

Merton, Thomas. *No Man is an Island*. New York: Harcourt, 1978.

Miller, Donald E. *Reinventing American Protestantism: Christianity in the New Millennium*. Berkley, Calif.: University of California Press.

Miller, Park Hays. *The New Testament Church, Its Teaching and Its Scriptures*. Philadelphia, Pa.: The Westminster Press, 1939.

Morgan, G. Campbell. *The Birth of the Church: An Exposition of the Second Chapter of Acts*. Old Tappan, N.J.: Fleming H. Revell Company, 1968.

Morgan, Robert J. *On This Day*. Nashville, Tenn.: Thomas Nelson. 1997.

Murray, Ian H. *Spurgeon Vs. Hyper-Calvinism*. Carlisle, Pa.: The Banner of Truth Trust, 1995.

Nee, Watchman. *Further Talks on the Church Life*. Los Angeles, Calif.: The Stream Publishers, 1969.

Nee. *The Glorious Church*. Taipei, Taiwan: The Gospel Book Room, 1968.

Nee. *The Normal Christian Church Life*. Washington, D.C.: International Students Press, 1962.

Nee. *Spiritual Authority*. New York: Christian Fellowship Publishers, Inc., 1972.

Nee. *The Spiritual Man*. Volume 2. New York: Christian Fellowship Publishers, Inc., 1968.

The New Dictionary of Theology. Edited by Sinclair B. Ferguson, David F. Wright and J. I. Packer. Downers Grove, Ill.: InterVarsity Press, 1988.

The New International Dictionary of the Christian Church. Edited by J. D. Douglas. Grand Rapids, Mich.: Zondervan Publishing House, 1974.

The New Schaff-Herzog Encyclopedia of Religious Knowledge. Edited by Phillip Schaff and Johann Herzog. Grand Rapid, Mich.: Baker Books. 1977 reprint.

Oden, Thomas C. *Interpretation: A Bible Commentary for Teaching and Preaching, First and Second Timothy and Titus. James*. Edited by James Luther Mays. Louisville, Ky.: John Knox Press.

Owen, John. *The Works of John Owen*, Vol. 15. Edinburgh, Scotland: The Banner of Truth, 1965.

Packer, J. I. *Freedom and Authority*. Oakland, Calif.: International Council on Biblical Inerrancy, 1981.

Paul, Robert S. *The Church In Search Of Its Self*. Wm. B. Eerdmans Publishing Company, 1972.

Perspectives on the World Christian Movement., A Reader. Edited by Ralph D. Winter and Steven C. Hawthorne. Pasadena, Calif.: William Carey Library, 1981.

Petersen, Jim. *Church Without Walls: Moving Beyond Traditional Boundaries.* Colorado Springs, Colo.: Navpress, 1992.

Peterson, Eugene. *Under the Predictable Planet.* Grand Rapids, Mich.: Wm. B. Eerdmans Publishing Company.

Pethrus, Lewi. *Christian Church Discipline.* Translated from the Swedish by Paul B. Peterson. Chicago, Ill.: Philadelphia Book Concern, 1944.

Piper, John. *Let the Nations Be Glad.* Grand Rapids, Mich.: Baker Books.

Radmacher, Earl D. *What the Church Is All About: A Biblical and Historical Study.* Chicago, Ill.: Moddy Press, 1978.

Ramm, Bernard. *The Pattern of Authority.* Grand Rapids, Mich.: Wm. B. Eerdmans Publishing Co., 1957.

Richard, Chairman George W. *The Nature of the Church.* A Report of the American Theological Committee of the Continuation Committee, World Conference on Faith and Order. Chicago, Ill.: Willett, Clark & Company, 1945.

Richards, Lawrence O. and Clyde Hoeldtke. *A Theology of Church Leadership.* Grand Rapids, Mich.: Zondervan Publishing House, 1980.

Rigg, Rev. James H. *A Comparative View of Church Organisations, Primitive and Protestant.* London: Charles H. Kelly, 1891.

Robertson, Archibald Thomas. *A Grammar of the Greek New Testament.* Nashville, Tenn.: Broadman, 1934.

Robertson. *Word Pictures in the New Testament: the Epistles of Paul.* Vol. IV. Nashville, Tenn.: Broadman Press.

Robinson, William. *The Biblical Doctrine of the Church.* St. Louis, Mo.: The Bethany Press, 1948.

Ross, A. Hastings. *The Church-Kingdom.* Lectures on Congregationalism, delivered on the Southworth Foundation in the

Andover Theological Seminary, 1882-1886. Boston, Mass.: Congregational Sunday School and Publishing Society, 1887.

Rouner, Arthur A., Jr. *The Congregational Way of Life.* Oak Creek, Wis.: Hammersmith-Breithhaupt Printing Co., 1960 and 1972.

Sanders, J. Oswald. *Spiritual Leadership.* Chicago, Ill.: Moody Press, 1967. Sasucy, Robert L. *The Church In God's Program.* Chicago, Ill.: Moody Press, 1972.

The Schaff-Herzog Encyclopedia. Edited by Phillip Schaff and Johann Herzog. New York: Funk and Wagnalls, 1883.

Schaller, Lyle E. *The Pastor and the People: Building a New Partnership for Effective Ministry.* Nashville, Tenn.: Abingdon Press, 1973.

Scheidler, Bill. *The New Testament Church and Its Ministries.* Portland, Ore.: Bible Press, 1980.

Scott, Earnest F. *The Nature of the Early Church.* New York: Charles Scribner's Sons, 1941.

Seiss, J. A. *The Apocalypse.* Grand Rapids, Mich.: Zondervan, 1957.

Selden. *The Story of the Christian Centuries.* Grand Rapids, Mich.: Fleming H. Revell Publishing.

Shelley, Bruce L. *Conservative Baptists: A Story of Twentieth-Century Dissent.* Denver, Colo.: Golden Bell Press, 1960.

Shelley. *Theology for Ordinary People.* Downers Grove, Ill.: Inter-Varsity Press, 1993.

Shelley, Bruce and Marshall Shelley. *The Consumer Church.* Downers Grove, Ill.: Inter-Varsity Press, 1992.

Shelley, Marshall. *Well-Intentioned Dragons: Ministering to Problem People in the Church.* Dallas, Tex.: Word Publishing, 1985.

Smith, David L. *All God's People: A Theology of the Church.* Wheaton, Ill.: A Bridgepoint Book, the academic imprint of Victor Books/Scripture Press Publications, Inc., 1996.

Snyder, Howard A. *Wine Skins: The Problem of Church Structure in a Technological Age*. Downers Grove, Ill.: Inter-Varsity Press, 1975.

Snyder. *The Community of the King*. Downers Grove, Ill.: Inter-Varsity Press, 1977.

Snyder. *Liberating the Church: The Ecology of Church & Kingdom*. Downers Grove, Ill.: Inter-Varsity Press, 1983.

Sproul, R. C. *Choosing My Religion*. Grand Rapids, Mich.: Baker Book House, 1995.

Stott, John R.W. *Guard the Truth: the Message of I and II Timothy & Titus*. Downers Grove, Ill.: Inter-Varsity Press.

Stott. *The Message of 2 Timothy: Guard the Gospel*. Downers Grove, Ill.: Inter-Varsity Press.

Stott. *The Preacher's Portrait*. Grand Rapids, Mich.: Wm. B. Eerdmans Publishing Company, 1961.

Strauch, Alexander. *Biblical Eldership: An Urgent Call to Restore Biblical Church Leadership*. Littleton, Colo.: Lewis and Roth Publishers, 1995.

Strong, Augustus Hopkins. *Systematic Theology: A Compendium Designed for the Use of Theological Students*. Three Volumes in One. Valley Forge, Pa.: The Judson Press.

Swetland, Kenneth L. *The Hidden World of the Pastor: Case Studies on Personal Issues of Real Pastors*. Grand Rapids, Mich.: Baker Books, 1995.

Theology & Authority. Edited by Richard Penaskovic. Peabody, Mass.: Hendrickson Publishers, 1987.

Thiessen, Arden. *The Work of the Pastor*. A Paper for Pastoral Theology at Steinbach Bible College, 1990.

Thiessen, Henry C. *Lectures in Systematic Theology*. Revised by Vernon D. Doerksen.
Grand Rapids, Mich.: Wm. B. Eerdmans Publishing Company, 1949, 1977.

Thornbury, John. *The Doctrine of the Church*. Lewisburg, Pa.:

Heritage Publishers, 1971.

Trench, R. C. *Synonyms of the New Testament.* Grand Rapids, Mich.: Wm. B. Eerdmans Publishing Company.

Trigg, Joseph W. and William L. Sachs. *Of One Body: Renewal Movements in the Church.* Atlanta, Ga.: John Knox Press, 1986.

Van Gelder, Craig. *The Essence of the Church. A Community Created by the Spirit.* Grand Rapids, Mich.: Baker Book House.

Vine, W.E., Unger, Merrill F., and White, William, Jr. *Vine's Complete Expository Dictionary of Old and New Testament Words.* Nashville, Tenn.: Thomas Nelson Publishers, 1985.

Walker, Williston. *The Creeds and Platforms of Congregationalism.* Philadelphia, Pa.: Pilgrim Press, 1969.

Walker. *A History of the Christian Church.* New York: Charles Scribner's Sons, 1924.

White, Jerry. *The Church & the Parachurch: An Uneasy Marriage.* Portland, Ore.: Multnomah Press, 1983.

Witherow, Thomas. *The Apostolic Church—Which is it?* Issued by the Publications Committee of the Free Presbyterian Church of Scotland. London: Morrison and Gibb Limited, 1967.

Wordsworth, John. *The Ministry of Grace—Studies in the Early Church History with Reference to Present Problems.* New York: Longman's Green and Co., 1901.

Working Your Way to the Nations: A Guide to Effective Tentmaking. Edited by Jonathan Lewis. Pasadena, Calif.: William Carey Library, 1993.

Wray, Daniel E. *The Importance of the Local Church.* Cheltenham, England: Taylor, Young Ltd., 1985.

Zacharias, Ravi. *Jesus Among Other Gods.* Nashville, Tenn.: Word Publishing, 2000.